SELE

SRI SANK

SELECT WORKS
OF
SRI SANKARACHARYA

SANSKRIT TEXT AND
ENGLISH TRANSLATION

TRANSLATED BY
S. VENKATARAMANAN

FOREWORD BY
K. BALASUBRAMANIA IYER, B.A., B.L.

PILGRIMS

PILGRIMS PUBLISHING
◆ Varanasi ◆

Select Works of Sri Sankaracharya
Translated by S. Venkataramanan

Published by:
PILGRIMS PUBLISHING

An imprint of:
PILGRIMS BOOK HOUSE
(Distributors in India)
B 27/98 A-8, Nawabganj Road
Durga Kund, Varanasi-221010, India
Tel: 91-542- 2314060,
Fax: 91-542- 2312456
E-mail: pilgrims@satyam.net.in
Website: www.pilgrimsbooks.com

Copyright © 2005, Pilgrims Publishing
All Rights Reserved

Cover design by Asha Mishra

ISBN: 81-7769-301-8

Printed in India at Pilgrim Press Pvt. Ltd. Lalpur Varanasi

PREFACE TO THE NEW EDITION

Sri Sankaracharya is famous throughout India as the great philosopher who reawakened interest in the ancient ideas contained in the six 'samayas', the six systems of Hindu philosophy. Such ideas are found across the great swathe of the subcontinent, from Holy Badrinath in the Himalayas to Tamil Nadu in the southern tropics.

Often referred to as 'Bhagavadpada', he is one of the greatest philosophers and spiritual teachers of mankind. It is not known when these verses were first written. It is believed that they emanated from him at a time of moral decline in religious ideas and after or during the period when Buddhism began to be influenced by liberal ideas. The demise of the pure Theravada or Hinayana Buddhism occurred when Tantric ideas developed, perhaps as early as the 7th century AD and up until the 11th century. The exact truth remains clouded in mist and is mostly mere speculation.

The outstanding contribution of Sri Sankaracharya is that he opened the way for the Hindu revival in the wake of the moral decline. Regarded by many as a saint, Sri Sankaracharya has a clear vision of life, its ills and its many uncompromising choices. He shows no obvious preference for the dominant Hindu deities, those gods that represent the differing themes of life's actions, hopes and inevitabilities.

As Radhakrishnan says, *"he destroyed many an old dogma, not by violently attacking it, but by quietly suggesting something more reasonable, which was at the same time more spiritual too."*

Translated by S. Venkataramanan, this book has chosen some of his more famous treatises and gives the verses in both Sanskrit and English. The main books are his Hymn to Hari, Direct Realisation, The Century of Verses, Knowledge of Self and Definition of One's Own Self.

Sri Sankaracharya's great themes are just as relevant today, and have withstood the test of time. His reigniting of Hindu philosophical ideas has given back to India that which might have been lost in the quagmire of religious decline.

Bob Gibbons
Siân Pritchard-Jones
Kathmandu 2004

CONTENTS

PREFACE

THE main object of this publication is to present, in simple English, some of the works of Sri Sankaracharya in which he tried to expound, in a popular style the philosophy of the Non-Dualistic Vedanta of which he was the well-known founder. With this view the present translation has been rendered free of technical words and phrases, and in some instances, literal and technical accuracy has been purposely sacrificed in order to make the translation readable and comprehensible by itself independently of the text. It is however hoped that the juxtaposition of the Sanskrit text and the English translation will serve the double object of enabling the student of Sanskrit to understand the text better and to correct, by a reference to the text, any defect of expression in the translation as an inevitable result of the attempt to garb it in a popular style. To those that have had no training in metaphysics or dialectics and have neither the leisure nor the capacity to read the original standard works of Sankara,—mostly elaborate commentaries on the Vedanta aphorisms, the Bhagavad-gita and the Upanishads—a publication of this kind should be specially helpful for a proper

understanding of the broad outline of
Sankara's philosophy of non-Dualism.
The main feature of that philosophy, as
will be apparent from a study of the
following pages, may be summed up very
briefly as follows: *Samsara* or phenomenal
existence, whose main factor is the bondage of births and deaths in succession
is unreal and is the result of illusion,—
the ignorance by which the only and
absolute reality, the Supreme Self is mistaken for the unreal world, in the same
way as a rope may be mistaken for a
serpent in the dusk of the evening. Both
bondage and liberation are thus illusory,
for, since there is no real bondage at all,
how can there be a liberation from it?
Yet, liberation or *moksha* is relatively
spoken of and can only result from a
thorough knowledge of the reality behind
and beyond and underneath and within
the unreal. Sankara emphasises the fact
that such knowledge is not a mere
theoretical one which can be gathered
from books or lectures, but is of the
nature of direct realisation or actual
experience. The sole source of this
knowledge is a clear and accurate understanding of the Vedic text "That thou
art," but, however much one may analyse
its meaning by means of his own reason
or with the aid of commentaries, the
direct realisation of the self cannot take

place unless the Vedic text in question
reaches the student through the mouth
of a spiritual teacher (the *guru*). It is
then, and only then that the disciple realises in a flash, as it were, " I am Brahman," the individual soul is seen, at all
times and in all conditions, to be identical with the Supreme Self, and the knowledge springs up that all this is indeed
the Self and there is naught but the Self.
This is the highest goal of spiritual
endeavour, the *moksha* or liberation of the
Vedanta philosophy. Further detail
would be out of place in a short preface
of this kind, but the translator feels
bound to call attention to one very
prominent teaching of Sankara which
will be evident from a perusal of the
present publication,—namely, that devotion to a personal God (*Saguna Brahman*)
is not inconsistent with the true Vedanta
philosophy, but, on the other hand,
spiritual perfection of liberation is
impossible without the grace of God
attainable by devotion and the grace of
the Master (*guru*) who alone can reveal
the true nature of the Self to the ardent
aspirant for the Absolute that is beyond
all word and thought.

THE TRANSLATOR

FOREWORD

I have great pleasure in writing a Foreword to this book and I am grateful to my esteemed friend, Mr. G.A. Natesan for having asked me to do so. Mr. Natesan, in the course of a distinguished career as a journalist, publisher and public worker, has been rendering very commendable service to the cause of Indian culture by the publication of selections and abridgments from the ancient Indian classics with good and accurate English translations of them. In fact, he has been a pioneer in this field of useful activity and richly deserves the warm praise of all lovers of our culture. Not the least among them is the present one.

The great Shankaracharya, known even in his own day with the honorific appellation of 'Bhagavatpada' is one of the greatest philosophers and spiritual teachers of mankind that the world has produced. He has made a profound and lasting contribution to the world's philosophic and religious thought. His inspiration and influence have been very great and abiding in his own country and have also been felt in a very marked degree in the West. I remember in the tenth session of the All India Philosophical Congress in 1934, presided over

by Dr. Mackenzie, the eminent philosophers Eastern and Western, assembled
there, voted unanimously with great
enthusiasm for a portrait of Shankara as
one of the great philosophers of the
world. Scholars differ greatly as regards
the age in which he lived, the dates
ranging from the second or third century
B. C. to the 8th or 9th century A. D. and
it is not possible to come to a definite
conclusion upon the evidences at present
available. But one thing can, with
certainty, be stated from the impressions
gathered from the internal evidence in
his works and from the traditional
accounts of his life and achievements,
that he was born during a very distracted
and unsettled period in the history of
Indian thought and culture. He, most
probably, should have lived at a time
when the pristine ethical purity and all-
pervading influence of Buddhism in
India was rapidly on the decline and, as
a result, there was great chaos and
confusion. Innumerable cults and sects
arose and divided the minds of men.
Corrupt practices and crude superstitions
masqueraded in the name of religion and
attracted many followers. Tradition
records that there were seventy-two
cults and sects during Shankara's period,
besmirching the fair name of India's
ancient noble religion and culture. It

was Shri Shankaracharya's marvellous hurricane campaign from Kashmere and Nepal in the North to Cape Comorin in the South—a campaign not of the sword, spelling ruin and destruction, but of intellectual conquest, peaceful persuasion, and loving propaganda that led to the victorious establishment of the unity and purity of enlightened Hindu thought and culture and the banishment of many superstitions, and corrupt practices and rites. He based his doctrines upon the fundamental truths experienced by the immortal seers of our race. The Kapalika, the Shakta and others like them fell before the sledge-hammer blows of his irresistible logic and were absorbed into one fold by his over-flowing kindness and his universal tolerance. The ancient well known six systems of Hindu theism known as the six samayas re-emerged, purged of all ex-crescences which crept into them during this dark age. Hence it is, that tradition refers to Shri Shankaracharya as 'the establisher of the shanmathas.' Where-ever we may go in India, whether to Bhadrinath and Amarnath on the snow-clad uplands of the Himalayas or to Kanyakumari and Tirichendur in the extreme south of India, we see still to-day enduring evidences of his enlightened reforming zeal and spiritual inspiration.

He devoted a great part of his energy to
the composition of beautiful stotras, in
praise of the supreme deities of the six
samayas for popular use in our daily
prayers, and they form a vital part of
Shankara's works that we have now got.
In these poems, we can enjoy his many-
sided personality as the devout adherent
of everyone of these samayas from his
standpoint of the unified and comprehensive conception of them. Without the
slightest tinge of partiality or preference,
he has adopted the stotras to the spirit
and technique of the various modes of
worship of these six samayas. He is at
once, an ardent devotee of Shiva in the
Sivanandalahari, a pious worshipper of
Vishnu in the Vishnu Padadikesanta
stotras, a humble servant of Parasakthi
in the Soundarya Lahari and a devoted
follower of Skanda and Ganapathi in the
poems in their praise. His stotras breathe
an intense religious fervour and infuse
the ecstasy and pathos of Bhakti and,
what is rare, are suffused with the spirit
of tolerance for the different angles of
vision of the earnest seeker for the God-
head. We see in them not the intellectual aristocrat or the disputing scholiast or
the thundering reformer but the devoted
supplicant at the feet of the Lord who, in
his infinite wisdom, takes many forms
suited to the varied mental equipment

and differing tastes of his devotees. We
find him therein denouncing in strong
terms the dissipation of the intellect,
energy and effort of man in the acquisi-
tion of book-learning and in fruitless
logic-chopping disputation. He proclaims
boldly the unpalatable truth " Nahi Nahi
Rakshathi Dukring Karane " and "Vritha
Kantakshobham Vahasi Tarka Vachasa".
To him, religion is realisation, not learning or dialectic.

With the aid of his wonderful spiritual
insight, his gigantic intellect, his intui-
tive genius, his profound and all-
comprehensive learning and his subtle
penetrating logic, he constructed the
many-mansioned edifice of Vedanta and
rested it on everlasting foundations.
Though the great Badarayana and
Gaudapada preceded him in evolving the
Vedantic thought, it was Shri Shankara
that established the Vedanta as the
prince among the darsanas of Indian
philosophy. Through his marvellous
Bhashya on the Brahma Sutras and his
lucid and masterly exposition of the
meaning of the Upanishads and his clear
and forcible commentary on the Gita and
through his simple and easy enunciation
of Vedantic doctrines in his prakaranas,
he formulated and popularised the truths
of the Vedanta and brought them home
to the millions of his countrymen. He

travelled ceaselessly throughout the length and breadth of India in an age when travelling was by no means easy or quick and even walked long distances barefooted and clad in the yellow robes of renunciation and spread his enlightened thought to all the masses. In his all too short life, he worked incessantly for the uplift and spiritual welfare of his countrymen and devoted all his energy to the service of humanity. His loving disciple, Padmapada, bears eloquent testimony in the Panchapadika to the fame and popularity of his great Acharya and to the wholesale dedication of his life for the sake of Lokanugraha, and describes in beautiful verse how people flocked to him from all quarters to hear the mellifluous flow of wisdom from his lips.

Though some of his important doctrines and conclusions are challenged by the other schools of Indian philosophy the main underlying currents of thought which distinguish the Vedanta as the foremost and distinct darsana have been recognised by them all. It is, indeed, profitable at the present day to emphasise this vital aspect of Shri Shankara's work as a philosopher, as we are apt to lose sight of it in the maze of polemical literature that has grown since his day between the three great schools of Vedanta philosophy which has only brought to the fore the keen differences among them. The doctrine of the self-evident validity of the Sruti Pramana, and the consequential principle of the supreme authority of the Prasthana Trayas (Upanishad, Brahma sutras and Gita), the doctrine of an ever-existent, unchanging Atma, the acceptance of Iswara as the first cause of the Universe as established by the sruti and not merely by anumana or inference and the theory of Ananda or positive happiness in Moksha as contrasted with the negative view of dukha nivritti of the naiyayika, vaiseshika, sankhya, patanjala and prabhakara schools of Indian Philosophy and self-luminosity and the sentient blissful nature of Jiva and its characteristic of doer and enjoyer—these and many more are common to all the three schools of Vedanta philosophy. All these owe their clear elucidation to the genius and masterful exposition of this great world-teacher. Even the great doctrine of Maya, always associated with his name, has been misunderstood as importing the theory of illusion and he has been sometimes denounced as a Crypto-Buddhist (Pracchanna Bauddha). But it is well to remember that Shankara strongly refutes the sunya vada of Buddhist philosophy, that nothing exists, neither matter nor mind, as well as the Kshanika Vada, that nothing exists for

more moments than one and the Vigna-
vada or the theory of subjectivism, the
denial of the externality of the world to
the thinking subject. The practical
utility of the Maya doctrine in its
bearing upon life consists in its efficacy
for developing the spirit of unity by
realizing that differences are unreal. In
fact, of the three kinds of Bheda, namely
Sajatiya, Vijatiya and Svagata Bheda into
which all differences in the world can be
classified, Shankara would reject all the
three as untrue, while Ramanuja would
discard the first two and Madhva would
refute the first.

Above all, the great services done by
Shankara is his method of approach
in the discussion and solution of the
problems of philosophy. He laid stress
on anubhava or integral experience, as
the final test of the truth or correctness
of any solution and on the acceptance of
sruti as the record of the religious
experience of the immortal seers of our
race. He would not pin his faith on the
validity of the conclusions of the finite
logical intellect of man. He would often
denounce the 'Sugata Samaya' (Buddhist
philosophy) for following the method of
implicitly accepting the dictates of one's
own intellect as the ultimate truth. He
believed in flawless reasoning as condu-
cive to the proper interpretation of sruti

and of anubhava and accepted the rigo-
rous standards of logic in the elucidation
of spiritual truths. He maintained a
scrupulous intellectual honesty and rested
his conclusions upon well-known and
authentic scriptural authority and on
accurate quotations therefrom. In the
enunciation of his doctrines and in his
refutations of the theories of other
darsanas he exhibited a calm, sober,
reasonable and just attitude and as
Sir Radhakrishnan says ' he destroyed
many an old dogma not by violently
attacking it but by quietly suggesting
something more reasonable which was at
the same time more spiritual too.' He
rarely criticised without mastering fully
their intricacies, details and technique
the other systems of philosophy and
seldom indulged in vituperative language
or in attributing motives to his oppon-
ents. In one place in his writings where
he exhibited an unusual warmth in criti-
cising the theory of the Tarkika he
gently apologises for this lapse by stating
that he did not indulge in criticism for
its own sake but for the sake of the pur-
suit and discovery of truth. He was
master of a wonderful style and even
those who criticised strongly his views
admired the power, lucidity, terseness,
suggestiveness and beauty of his prose.
In his own school of Advaita Vedanta he

held a unique place and unlike the case of the other darsanas, his doctrines and theories have been followed with respect and admiration, but never departed from, by any of the brilliant galaxy of Advaita teachers and writers that have succeeded him till the present day.

In him, we have the unique combination of the saint and the ascetic, the scholar and the poet, the philosopher, religious reformer, and man of action. It is refreshing to read the beautiful account of his intense love and devotion to his mother in striking contrast to his cold asceticism. In spite of the many centuries that have elapsed since his passing away. his great inspiration and tradition have been kept fully alive even to-day through the influence of the great Mutts he established for the spiritual welfare of succeeding generations of his countrymen and by the illustrious succession of disciples who have adorned the headship of these Mutts and shed their spiritual lustre upon their fellowmen.

He taught mankind to love truth, respect reason, practise tolerance and realize the purpose of life. None can deny his rightful place among the immortals of the world.

" Ashrama"
MYLAPORE.   K. BALASUBRAMANIA IYER.

SELECT WORKS

OF

Sri Sankaracharya

॥ हरिस्तुतिः ॥

HYMN TO HARI

स्तोष्ये भक्त्या विष्णुमनादिं जगदादिं
यस्मिन्नेतत्संसृतिचक्रं भ्रमतीत्थम् ।
यस्मिन्दृष्टे नश्यति तत्संसृतिचक्रं
तं संसारध्वान्तविनाशं हरिमीडे ॥ १ ॥

I praise, with devotion, the All-
pervading (Vishnu), Who Himself without origin, is the origin of the universe,
in whom this wheel of *samsara** revolves in
this wise, and realising Whom, this wheel
of *samsara* is destroyed—that Hari, the
destroyer of the darkness of *samsara*, I
praise.   (1)

---

*Phenomenal existence; the succession of births
and deaths.

707—2

यस्यैकांशादित्थमशेषं जगदेतत्
    प्रादुर्भूतं येन पिनद्धं पुनरित्थम् ।
येन व्याप्तं येन विबुद्धं सुखदुःखैः
    तं संसारध्वान्तविनाशं हरिमीडे ॥ २ ॥

Him, from a single aspect of Whom
this whole universe has sprung into
existence, by Whom again it is held
together in this manner, by Whom it is
pervaded and by Whom it is illumined
through pleasure and pain,—that Hari,
the destroyer of the darkness of *samsara*,
I praise.   (2)

सर्वज्ञो यो यत्र हि सर्वः सकलो यो
    यश्चानन्दोऽनन्तगुणो यो गुणधामा ।
यश्चाव्यक्तो व्यस्तसमस्तः सदसद्यः
    तं संसारध्वान्तविनाशं हरिमीडे ॥ ३ ॥

Him, Who is all-knowing, Who is
indeed all and perfect, who is bliss itself,
Who resides in the qualities* and has
therefore endless attributes, Who is
Unmanifest   that   differentiates   the

---

* Sattva, Rajas and Tamas.

undifferentiated, and Who is both real
and the unreal,—that Hari, the destroyer
of the darkness of *samsara*, I praise.　　(3)

यस्मादन्यन्नास्त्यपि नैवं परमार्थं
　　दृश्यादन्यो निर्विषयज्ञानमयत्वात् ।
ज्ञातृज्ञानज्ञेयविहीनोऽपि सदा ज्ञः
　　तं संसारध्वान्तविनाशं हरिमीडे ॥ ४ ॥

There is naught else than Him; yet,
this universe is not his real nature. He is
not the objective world, for He is of the
nature of non-objective consciousness.
And though He is devoid of the distinction of the knower, knowledge and the
known, He is nevertheless always the
knower,—that Hari, the destroyer of the
darkness of *samsara*, I praise.　　(4)

आचार्येभ्यो लब्धसुसूक्ष्माच्युततत्त्वाः
　　वैराग्येणाभ्यासबलाच्चैव दृढिम्ना ।
भक्त्यैकाग्र्यध्यानपरा यं विदुरीशं
　　तं संसारध्वान्तविनाशं हरिमीडे ॥ ५ ॥

Him who is realised as the Supreme
Lord by those who, having learnt from
proper preceptors the extremely subtle

nature of the Immutable, are engaged in
the contemplation of the ultimate Unity
with the help of renunciation, constant
meditation and firm devotion,—that Hari,
the destroyer of the darkness of *samsara*,
I praise.   (5)

प्राणानायम्योमिति चित्तं हृदि रुध्वा
　　नान्यत्स्मृत्वा तत्पुनरत्रैव विलाप्य ।
क्षीणे चित्ते भाद्दशिरस्मीति विदुर्यं
　　तं संसार्ध्वान्तविनाशं हरिमीडे ॥ ६ ॥

Him who is realised as "I am the self-
resplendent Self" when, by the control
of the life-forces, the mind is confined
within the heart amidst the repetition of
the sound Om and, all other memory
being excluded, is merged therein and
is finally dissolved,—that Hari, the
destroyer of the darkness of *samsara*,
I praise.   (6)

यं ब्रह्माल्यं देवमनन्यं परिपूर्णं
　　हृत्स्थं भक्तैलैभ्यमजं सूक्ष्ममतवर्यंम् ।
ध्यात्वाऽऽत्मस्थं ब्रह्मविदो यं विदुरीशं
　　तं संसार्ध्वान्तविनाशं हरिमीडे ॥ ७ ॥

Him Whom the knowers of Brahman
realise by meditation as the Supreme
Lord within themselves known as
Brahman, as the secondless. infinite,
unborn, subtle, inscrutable Resplendence
residing in the heart and attainable only
by devotees,—that Hari, the destroyer of
the darkness of *samsara*, I praise.　(7)

मात्रातीतं खात्मविकासात्मविबोधं
　ज्ञेयातीतं ज्ञानमयं हृद्युपलभ्य ।
भावग्राह्यानन्दमनन्यं च विदुर्यं
　तं संसारध्वान्तविनाशं हरिमीडे ॥ ८ ॥

Him Who is understood as the unsur-
passable bliss realisable only by the
spirit by those who perceive within their
own hearts. That which is beyond the
senses, being realisable only by the
expansion of the individual self, and
beyond the cognisable, being cognition
itself,—that Hari, the destroyer of the
darkness of *samsara*, I praise.　(8)

यद्यद्वेद्यं वस्तु सतत्त्वं विषयाख्यं
　तत्तद्द्वैवेति विदित्वा तदहं च ।

ध्यायन्त्येवं यं सनकाद्या मुनयोऽजं
तं संसारध्वान्तविनाशं हरिमीडे ॥ ९ ॥

Him Whom, the Unborn sages like
Sanaka meditate upon by understanding
that every object of perception has an
underlying reality and is identical with
Brahman and by realising "I am That",
that Hari, the destroyer of the darkness
of *samsara*, I praise.   (9)

यद्ध्द्वेयं तत्तदहं नेति विहाय
स्वात्मज्योतिर्ज्ञानमयानन्दमवाप्य ।
तस्मिन्नस्मीत्यात्मविदो यं विदुरीशं
तं संसारध्वान्तविनाशं हरिमीडे ॥ १० ॥

Him Whom the knowers of SELF know
as the Supreme Lord "in whom I am" by
eliminating as not-I whatever is perceptible, and by realising that bliss which is
self-resplendent consciousness,—that Hari,
the destroyer of the darkness of *samsara*,
I praise.   (10)

हित्वा हित्वा दृश्यमशेषं सविकल्पं
मत्वा शिष्टं भादृशिमात्रं गगनाभम् ।

त्यक्त्वा देहं यं प्रविशन्त्यच्युतभक्ताः
तं संसारध्वान्तविनाशं हरिमीडे ॥ ११ ॥

Him in Whom the devotees of the
Immutable, forsaking their bodies, merge
themselves by realising Him as the pure
self-resplendent SELF, infinite like space,
as That which alone remains when all
that is cognisable and differentiated is
eliminated step by step,—that Hari, the
destroyer of the darkness of *samsara*, I
praise.   **(11)**

सर्वत्रास्ते सर्वशरीरी न च सर्वः
    सर्वं वेत्त्येवेह न यं वेत्ति च सर्वः ।
सर्वत्रान्तर्यामितयेत्थं यमयन्यः
    तं संसारध्वान्तविनाशं हरिमीडे ॥ १२ ॥

Him Who is in all, Whose body is this
all, and yet Who not this all, Who knows
all, but Whom none knows at all, and
Who, as stated above, holds all this
together, being the inner spirit thereof,—
that Hari, the destroyer of the darkness
of *samsara*, I praise.   **(12)**

सर्वं दृष्ट्वा खात्मनि युक्त्या जगदेतत्
दृष्ट्वाऽऽत्मानं चैवमजं सर्वजनेषु ।
सर्वात्मैकोऽस्मीति विदुर्यं जनहृत्स्थं
तं संसारध्वान्तविनाशं हरिमीडे ॥ १३ ॥

Him Who is realised as "I am the One
that is the All" by those who see, by their
reason, all this universe as existing within themselves and their own self as the
Unborn residing in the heart of all
beings,—that Hari, the destroyer of the
darkness of *samsara*, I praise.   (13)

सर्वत्रैकः पश्यति जिघ्रयथ भुङ्क्ते
स्रष्टा श्रोता बुध्यति चेत्याहुरिमं यम् ।
साक्षी चास्ते कर्तृषु पश्यन्निति चान्ये
तं संसारध्वान्तविनाशं हरिमीडे ॥ १४ ॥

Him Who is described by some as the
One in all beings that sees and smells and
tastes and touches and hears and knows,
and by others as the witness that is the
seer in all doers,—that Hari, the destroyer
of the darkness of *samsara*, I praise.   (14)

पश्यन्शृण्वन्नत्र विजानन्नसयन्सं-
जिघ्रद्विभ्रद्देहमिमं जीवतयेत्थम् ।
इत्यात्मानं यं विदुरीशं विषयज्ञं
तं संसारध्वान्तविनाशं हरिमीडे ॥ १५ ॥

Him Who is realised as the Supreme
Lord the SELF that is the knower of
objects, Who sees and hears and knows
and tastes and smells and holds this body
together as the individual self therein,—
that Hari, the destroyer of the darkness
of *samsara*, I praise. (15)

जाग्रहृष्ट्वा स्थूलपदार्थानथ मायां
हृष्ट्वा स्वप्नेऽथापि सुषुप्तौ सुखनिद्राम् ।
इत्यात्मानं वीक्ष्य मुदाऽऽस्ते च तुरीये
तं संसारध्वान्तविनाशं हरिमीडे ॥ १६ ॥

He Who sees objects of gross matter in
the waking state, illusion in dream, and
blissful repose in deep sleep and Himself
in the fourth state and is happy,—that
Hari, the destroyer of the darkness of
samsara, I praise. (16)

पश्यन्नुद्धोऽप्यक्षर एको गुणभेदान्
नानाकारान्स्फाटिकवद्भाति विचित्रः ।

भिन्नश्छन्नश्छायमजः कर्मफलैर्यैः
तं संसारध्वान्तविनाशं हरिमीडे ॥ १७ ॥

Him Who though pure, imperishable,
one and unborn, nevertheless imposes
upon Himself* different qualities and
different shapes and, like crystal†, shines
variegated, differentiated and hidden by
the fruits of action—that Hari, the
destroyer of the darkness of *samsara*, I
praise.   (17)

ब्रह्माविष्णू रुद्रहुताशौ रविचन्द्रौ
इन्द्रो वायुर्यज्ञ इतीत्थं परिकल्प्य ।
एकं सन्तं यं बहुधाऽऽहुर्मतिभेदात्
तं संसारध्वान्तविनाशं हरिमीडे ॥ १८ ॥

Him Who is the one Reality, but Who
owing to the diversity of intellects, is
conventionally spoken of in various ways
as Brahma, Vishnu, Rudra, Fire, the Sun,
the Moon, Indra, Vayu (the God of Wind),
and sacrifice,—that Hari, the destroyer of
the darkness of *samsara*, I praise.   (18)

---

* Lit : Sees.   † Reflecting external colours.

सत्यं ज्ञानं शुद्धमनन्तं व्यतिरिक्तं
शान्तं गूढं निष्कलमानन्दमनन्यम् ।
इत्याहादौ यं वरुणोऽसौ भृगवेऽजं
तं संसारध्वान्तविनाशं हरिमीडे ॥ १९ ॥

Him, the Unborn, Whom, at the beginning of the Taittiriya-Upanishad,
Varuna explained to Bhrigu* as being
uncontradictable, conscious, pure, imperishable, transcendental unperturbed,
unperceivable without parts, blissful,
and without a second,—that Hari, the
destroyer of the darkness of *samsara*, I
praise.   (19)

कोशानेतान्पञ्च रसादीनतिहाय
ब्रह्मास्मीति स्वात्मनि निश्चित्य दृशिस्थम् ।
पित्रा शिष्टो वेद भृगुर्यं यजुरन्ते
तं संसारध्वान्तविनाशं हरिमीडे ॥ २० ॥

Him whom, as stated at the end of the
Taittiriya-Upanishad, Bhrigu, taught by
his father, realised as the witness in
everything after having determined
within himself "I am the Brahman beyond

* Son of Varuna.

these five sheaths of taste, etc.",*—that
Hari, the destroyer of the darkness of
samsara, I praise.   (20)

येनाविष्टो यस्य च शक्त्या यदधीनः
क्षेत्रज्ञोऽयं कारयिता जन्तुषु कर्तुः ।
कर्ता भोक्ताऽऽत्मात्र हि यच्छक्त्यधिरूढः
तं संसारध्वान्तविनाशं हरिमीडे ॥ २१ ॥

Him by Whose inspiration, by Whose
power,† and on whom depending, the
knower of the field‡ directs the active
principle in all creatures, and by Whose
power is impelled the self that is the doer
and enjoyer in this world,—that Hari, the
destroyer of the darkness of *samsara*, I
praise.   (21)

सृष्ट्वा सर्वं स्वात्मतयैवेत्थमतर्क्यं
व्याप्याधास्तन्तः कृत्स्नमिदं सृष्टमशेषम् ।
सच्च त्यचाभूत्परमात्मा स य एकः
तं संसारध्वान्तविनाशं हरिमीडे ॥ २२ ॥

---

* The five *kosas*, namely, annamaya, pranamaya,
manomaya, vijinanamaya and anandamaya.
  † Maya-sakti, the power of illusion.
  ‡ Kshetrajna, the individual conscious self.
  ‖ Chit-sakti, the power of intelligence.

Him, the one supreme SELF, Who
created all this indescribable universe
and Who fully permeates every part of
that creation, being identical therewith,
and thus becomes all that is manifest
and unmanifest,–that Hari, the destroyer
of the darkness of *samsara*, I praise. (22)

वेदान्तैश्चाध्यात्मिकशास्त्रैश्च पुराणैः

शास्त्रैश्चान्यैः सात्त्वततन्त्रैश्च पुराणैः ।

दृष्ट्वाऽधान्तश्चेतसि बुध्वा विविशुर्ये

तं संसारध्वान्तविनाशं हरिमीडे ॥ २३ ॥

Him Whom, by the help of the Vedantas, the sciences treating of the self, the
Puranas, the cults of Vishnu-worship and
other sciences, may have realised as the
Supreme Lord within their own selves
and, knowing thus, have merged themselves into him,—that Hari, the destroyer
of the darkness of *samsara*, I praise. (23)

श्रद्धाभक्तिध्यानशमाचैर्यैयतमानैः

ज्ञातुं शक्यो देव इहैवाशु य ईशः ।

दुर्विज्ञेयो जन्मशतैश्चापि विना तैः
तं संसाराध्वान्तविनाशं हरिमीडे ॥ २४ ॥

Him, the resplendent Lord, Who is
speedily realisable even in this world by
those who strive to seek him by means of
faith, devotion, meditation, self-control
and other expedients, but Who is hard
to realise even through hundreds of lives
for those who are devoid of those expedients,—that Hari, the destroyer of the
darkness of *samsara*, I praise.   (24)

यस्यातर्क्यं स्वात्मविभूतेः परमार्थं
सर्वं खल्विदयत्र निरुक्तं श्रुतिविद्भिः ।
तज्जादित्वादधिगतरङ्गाभमभिन्नं
तं संसाराध्वान्तविनाशं हरिमीडे ॥ २५ ॥

Him, the indescribable glory of Whose
manifestation has been defined by the
Vedic seers in the passage " All this
indeed is Brahman," that is, all this
being born of Him, being in Him and
dissolving in Him, is identical with Him,
like the waves of the ocean,—that Hari,
the destroyer of the darkness of *samsara*,
I praise.   (25)

दृष्ट्वा गीतास्वक्षरतत्त्वं विधिनाऽजं
भक्त्या गुर्व्यो लभ्य हृदिस्थं दृशिमात्रम् ।
ध्यात्वा तस्मिन्नस्यहमिमयत्र विदुर्यं
तं संसारध्वान्तविनाशं हरिमीडे ॥ २६ ॥

Him who is realised by intense devotion
as the unborn and indestructible
principle, the pure intelligence residing
as Witness in the heart, and by meditating "I am in Him," as taught in the
Gita and in the manner laid down therein,—that Hari, the destroyer of the darkness of *samsara*, I praise.   (26)

क्षेत्रज्ञत्वं प्राप्य विभुः पञ्चमुखैर्यो
भुङ्क्तेऽजस्रं भोग्यपदार्थान्प्रकृतिस्थः ।
क्षेत्रे क्षेत्रेऽप्स्विन्दुवदेको बहुधाऽऽस्ते
तं संसारध्वान्तविनाशं हरिमीडे ॥ २७ ॥

Him, the Infinite, Who, assuming the
condition of the individual self and
dwelling in nature, incessantly enjoys
the objects of enjoyment through the five
gateways of the senses, and Who, though
one, appears as different in different

bodies like the moon reflected in the
waters,—that Hari, the destroyer of the
darkness of *samsara*, I praise.   (27)

युक्त्याऽऽलोड्य व्यासवचांस्तत्र हि लभ्यः
    क्षेत्रक्षेत्रज्ञान्तरविद्धिः पुरुषाख्यः ।
योऽहं सोऽसौ सोऽस्म्यहमेवेति विदुर्यं
    तं संसारध्वान्तविनाशं हरिमीडे ॥ २८ ॥

Him Who is named Purusha and Who
is realised, even in this world, as " He
who is I is that Supreme Lord and I am
verily He " by those who intelligently
investigate the teachings of Vyasa* and
understand the distinction between the
field and the knower of the field,†—that
Hari, the destroyer of the darkness of
samsara, I praise.   (28)

एकीकृत्यानेकशरीरस्थमिमं झं
    यं विज्ञायेहैव स एवाशु भवन्ति ।
यस्मिन्लीना नेह पुनर्जन्म लभन्ते
    तं संसारध्वान्तविनाशं हरिमीडे ॥ २९ ॥

---

* The Brahma Sutras of Vyasa.
* Kshetra, the field or the body, and Kshetrajna,
the knower of the field or the individual self.

Him, the conscious principle residing
in innumerable bodies, Whose oneness
realising, men speedily become Himself
in this very life, and, in Whom merged,
they come no more to birth in this world,
—that Hari, the destroyer of the darkness of *samsara*, I praise, (29)

द्वन्द्वैकत्वं यच्च मधुब्राह्मणवाक्यैः

कृत्वा शक्रोपासनमासाद्य विभूत्या ।

योऽसौ सोऽयं सोऽस्म्यहमेवेति विदुर्यं

तं संसाराध्वान्तविनाशं हरिमीडे ॥ ३० ॥

Him Who is realised as "He that is
the Supreme Lord is I and I am verily
He" by those who understand the unity
in duality taught by the passages of the
Madhu-Brahmana* and attain a supre-
macy that exacts veneration even at the
hands of Indra,—that Hari, the destroyer
of the darkness of *samsara*, I praise. (30)

योऽयं देहे चेष्टयिताऽन्तःकरणस्थः

सूर्ये चासौ तापयिता सोऽस्म्यहमेव ।

---

* Brih. Up., II. 5.

इत्यात्मैक्योपासनया यं विदुरीशं
तं संसारध्वान्तविनाशं हरिमीडे ॥ ३१ ॥

Him Who is realised as the Supreme
Lord by those who meditate on the unity
of the SELF, as " He that, dwelling in the
mind, impels the body to action, He too
that, residing in the sun, causes him to
radiate heat, I am verily He,"—that Hari,
the destroyer of the darkness of *samsara*,
I praise.   (31)

विज्ञानांशोर्येस्य सतः शक्त्यधिरूढो
बुद्धेर्बुध्यत्यत्र बहिर्बोध्यपदार्थान् ।
नैवान्तःस्थं बुध्यति यं बोधयितारं
तं संसारध्वान्तविनाशं हरिमीडे ॥ ३२ ॥

Him, the ultimate reality, a spark of
Whose consciousness reflected in nature*
cognises the objects of cognition outside
the mind, but does not cognise Him that
dwells within the mind and inspires the
cognition,—that Hari, the destroyer of
the darkness of *samsara*, I praise.   (32)

---

i.e., the individual self.

कोऽयं देहे देव इतीत्थं सुविचार्य
  ज्ञाता श्रोता मन्त्रयिता चैष हि देवः ।
इत्यालोच्य ज्ञांश इहास्मीति विदुर्यं
  तं संसाराध्वान्तविनाशं हरिमीडे ॥ ३३ ॥

Him who is realised as "I am that conscious principle in this body" by those
who intelligently enquire "Who is this
Shining One in the body?" and deter-
mine that this Shining one is indeed the
knower, the hearer and the thinker,—
that Hari, the destroyer of the darkness
of *samsara*, I praise.   (33)

को ह्येवान्यादात्मनि न स्यादयमेष
  ह्येवानन्दः प्राणिति चापानिति चेति ।
इत्यस्तित्वं वक्त्युपपत्त्या श्रुतिरेषा
  तं संसाराध्वान्तविनाशं हरिमीडे ॥ ३४ ॥

Who indeed can live, if He does not
reside in the body? He alone, therefore,
is the Supreme Bliss and He is the
incoming and outgoing life. By such
reasoning does the Scripture* declare
that He is,—that Hari, the destroyer of
the darkness of *samsara*, I praise.   (34)

* The Taittiriya-Upanishad.

प्राणो वाऽहं वाक्श्रवणादीनि मनो वा
　　बुद्धिर्वाऽहं व्यस्त उताथापि समस्तः ।
इत्यालोच्य ज्ञप्तिरिहास्मीति विदुर्यं
　　तं संसारध्वान्तविनाशं हरिमीडे ॥ ३५ ॥

"Am I the vital energy*? Or Speech ?
Or the senses of hearing etc? Or the
mind †? Or the intellect? ‡ Am I a particular entity or the collective whole?"
Him Who, by thus meditating, is realised as "I am the conscious principle in
this body,"—that Hari, the destroyer of
the darkness of *samsara*, I praise.   (35)

नाहं प्राणो नैव शरीरं न मनोऽहं
　　नाहं बुद्धिर्नोहमहङ्कारधियौ च ।
योऽत्र ज्ञांशस्सोऽस्म्यहमेवेति विदुर्यं
　　तं संसारध्वान्तविनाशं हरिमीडे ॥ ३६ ॥

Him Who is realised as "I am not the
vital energy*, nor the body, nor the
mind†, nor the intellect‡, nor the ego§,
nor the understanding ‖, but am verily
He that the conscious principle in this

---

* Prana. † Manas, ‡ Buddhi, § Ahankara. ‖ Dhi.

body,"—that Hari, the destroyer of the
darkness of *samsara*, I praise.   (36)

सत्तामात्रं केवलविज्ञानमजं सत्
     सूक्ष्मं नित्यं तत्त्वमसीत्यात्मसुताय ।
साम्नामन्ते प्राह पिता यं विभुमाद्यं
     तं संसारध्वान्तविनाशं हरिमीडे ॥ ३७ ॥

Him Whom, in the Upanishad of the
Samaveda*, the father † explains to his
son ‡ as pure existence, pure consciousness, the unborn, the real, the transcendental, the eternal, the infinite, the first
cause, and by declaring "That thou art",
—that Hari, the destroyer of the darkness
of *samsara*, I praise.   (37)

मूर्तामूर्ते पूर्वमपोह्याथ समाधौ
     दृश्यं सर्वं नेति च नेतीति विहाय ।
चैतन्यांशे स्वात्मनि सन्तं च विदुर्यं
     तं संसारध्वान्तविनाशं हरिमीडे ॥ ३८ ॥

Him Who is realised as the ultimate
reality by those who, through perfect

---

*Chhandogya- Upanishad.   †Uddalaka.   ‡Svetaketu.

absorption of thought*, attain to the
knowledge of the conscious principle
within themselves by first excluding all
conditioned and unconditioned existence
and then eliminating all that is perceptible as "Not this", "Not this",—that Hari,
the destroyer of the darkness of *samsara*,
I praise.   (38)

ओतं प्रोतं यत्र च सर्वं गगनान्तं
  योऽस्थूलानण्वादिषु सिद्धोऽक्षरसंज्ञः ।
ज्ञाताऽतो यो नेत्युपलभ्यो न च वेद्यः
  तं संसाराध्वान्तविनाशं हरिमीडे ॥ ३९ ॥

Him Who is the warp and woof of the
web of this universe including the undifferentiated ether, Who, is established
under the designation of the Instructible
in such passages as "It is not gross, It is
not atomic etc.", Who can only be understood as "There is no knower but He,"
but Who is not the object of cognition,
—that Hari, the destroyer of the darkness
of *samsara*, I praise.   (39)

---

* Samadhi.

तावत्सर्वं सत्यमिवाभाति यदेतत्
    यावत्सोऽस्मीत्यात्मनि यो ज्ञो न हि दृष्टः ।
दृष्टे यस्मिन्सर्वमसत्यं भवतीदं
    तं संसारध्वान्तविनाशं हरिमीडे ॥ ४० ॥

Him, the Knower, without realising
Whom within one's self as "I am He,"
all this appears as real, but, who being
realised, all this becomes unreal,—that
Hari the destroyer of the darkness of
samsara, I praise.   (40)

रागामुक्तं लोहयुतं हेम यथाऽग्नौ
    योगाष्टाङ्गैरुज्ज्वलितज्ञानमयाग्नौ ।
दग्ध्वाऽऽत्मानं ज्ञं परिशिष्टं च विदुर्यं
    तं संसारध्वान्तविनाशं हरिमीडे ॥ ४१ ॥

Him Who is realised as the consciousness that ultimately remains when the
self that is not free from impurity is
burnt in the fire of knowledge kindled by
eightfold Yoga*, like gold alloyed with
iron in the furnace,—that Hari, the destroyer of the darkness of *samsara*, I
praise.   (41)

* Yama, Niyama, Asana, Pranayama, Pratyahara,
Dharana, Dhyana and Samadhi.

यं विज्ञानज्योतिषमाद्यं सुविभान्तं
हृद्यर्कन्द्वग्न्योकसमीक्ष्यं तटिदाभम् ।
भक्त्याऽऽराध्येहैव विशन्त्यात्मनि सन्तं
तं संसारध्वान्तविनाशं हरिमीडे ॥ ४२ ॥

Him Who is the resplendent light of
consciousness, the first cause, the praise-
worthy, Who shines like lightning within
the heart amidst the spheres of the sun,
moon and fire,* in Whom the sages, worshipping Him with devotion as the ultimate reality within their own selves,
merge themselves even in this life,—that
Hari, the destroyer of the darkness of
samsara, I praise.
(42)

पायाद्द्रक्कं खात्मनि सन्तं पुरुषं यो
भक्त्या स्तौतीयाङ्गिरसं विष्णुरिमं माम् ।
इत्यात्मानं खात्मनि संहृत्य सदैकः
तं संसारध्वान्तविनाशं हरिमीडे ॥ ४३ ॥

May He, the all-pervading (Vishnu),
protect this devotee who is an individual
self†existing in Himself, considering

---

*This is a technicality of the higher *Yoga*.
†Purusha.

"This devotee praises Me Who am the
essence of all organs with constant devotion and single-mindedness and with-
drawing himself within his own self"—
that Hari, the destroyer of the darkness
of *samsara*, I praise.   (43)

इत्थं स्तोत्रं भक्तजनेड्यं भवभीति-
    ध्वान्ताकार्भं भगवत्पादीयमिदं यः ।
विष्णोर्लोकं पठति श्रृणोति व्रजति ज्ञो
    ज्ञानं ज्ञेयं स्वात्मनि चाप्नोति मनुष्यः ॥ ४४ ॥

He who recites or hears this hymn of
the venerable teacher, valuable to devotees and resembling the sun in dispelling
the darkness of the fear of *samsara*,
attains the state of the All-pervading
(Vishnu) and, becoming a seer, realises
both knowledge and the object of knowledge* within himself.   (44)

॥ इति हरिस्तुतिः समाप्ता ॥

Thus ends the hymn to Hari.

---

* The Supreme Being.

॥ दशश्लोकी ॥

THE TEN-VERSED HYMN

न भूमिर्न तोयं न तेजो न वायुः

न खं नेन्द्रियं वा न तेषां समूहः ।

अनैकान्तिकत्वात्सुषुप्त्येकसिद्धः

तदेकोऽवशिष्टः शिवः केवलोऽहम् ॥ १ ॥

I am neither earth, nor water, nor fire, nor air, nor ether, nor sensory organ, nor the conglomeration of all these; for, all these are transient. I am He that alone remains in deep sleep, the secondless, uncontradictable* attributeless B l i s s (Siva).

(I)

न वर्णा न वर्णाश्रमाचारधर्माः

न मे धारणाध्यानयोगादयोऽपि ।

अनात्माश्रयाहम्ममाध्यासहानात्

तदेकोऽवशिष्टः शिवः केवलोऽहम् ॥ २ ॥

I am neither castes, nor the rules of caste, society and custom, nor for me are

---

* Lit. the ultimate remnant.

concentration, meditation, *Yoga* and
other practices; for, all this illusion of
"I" and "mine" is rooted in the not-self
and is therefore dispellable by the knowledge of the self. I am therefore the
secondless, uncontradictable, attributeless Bliss (Siva.) (2)

न माता पिता वा न देवा न लोकाः
न वेदा न यज्ञा न तीर्थं ब्रुवन्ति ।
सुषुप्तौ निरस्तातिशून्यात्मकत्वात्
तदेकोऽवशिष्टः शिवः केवलोऽहम् ॥ ३ ॥

I am neither mother, nor father, nor the
gods, nor the worlds, nor the *Vedas*, nor
sacrifices, nor any holy place; for, in
deep sleep I am [identical with Brahman
which however is] not absolute non-
existence. I am therefore the secondless,
uncontradictable attributeless B l i s s
(Siva). (3)

न साङ्ख्यं न शैवं न तत्पाञ्चरात्रं
न जैनं न मीमांसकादेर्मतं वा ।
विशिष्टानुभूत्या विशुद्धात्मकत्वात्
तदेकोऽवशिष्टः शिवः केवलोऽहम् ॥ ४ ॥

Neither the Sankhya doctrine, nor the
Saiva, nor the Pancharatra, nor the Jaina,

nor the Mimamsaka, nor any other, holds
good. For, by special realisation it is
revealed that my nature is absolutely
pure. I am therefore the secondless,
uncontradictable, nor attributeless Bliss
(Siva). (4)

न चोर्ध्वं न चाधो न चान्तर्ने बाह्यं
न मध्यं न तिर्यङ् न पूर्वा परा दिक् ।
वियद्व्यापकत्वादखण्डैकरूपः
तदेकोऽवशिष्टः शिवः केवलोऽहम् ॥ ५ ॥

I am neither above, nor below, nor
inside, nor outside, nor middle, nor
across, nor before, nor behind ; for I am
indivisible and one by nature and am all-
pervading like space. I am therefore the
secondless, uncontradictable, attributeless Bliss (Siva.) (5)

न शुक्लं न कृष्णं न रक्तं न पीतं
न कुब्जं न पीनं न ह्रस्वं न दीर्घम् ।
अरूपं तथा ज्योतिराकारकत्वात्
तदेकोऽवशिष्टः शिवः केवलोऽहम् ॥ ६ ॥

I am neither white, nor black, nor red,
nor yellow, nor bent, nor stout, nor short,
nor tall, nor even formless ; for I am of the

nature of self-resplendent consciousness.
I am therefore the secondless, uncontradictable, attributeless Bliss (Siva).   (6)

न शास्ता न शास्त्रं न शिष्यो न शिक्षा
    न च त्वं न चाहं न चायं प्रपञ्चः ।
स्वरूपावबोधो विकल्पासहिष्णुः
    तदेकोऽवशिष्टः शिवः केवलोऽहम् ॥ ७ ॥

There is neither teacher, nor science,
nor pupil, nor teaching, nor you (the
hearer), nor I (the speaker), nor this
empirical universe; for I am the consciousness of the reality, which does not
admit of differentiation. I am therefore
the secondless, uncontradictable, attributeless Bliss (Siva).   (7)

न जाग्रन्न मे स्वप्नको वा सुषुप्तिः
    न विश्वो न वा तैजसः प्राज्ञको वा ।
अविद्यात्मकत्वात्त्रयाणां तुरीयः
    तदेकोऽवशिष्टः शिवः केवलोऽहम् ॥ ८ ॥

For me there is neither waking nor
dream nor deep sleep, nor am I the self
conditioned by any of these three states
(*visva, taijasa* or *prajna*); for, all these

are of the nature of nescience, but I am
the fourth beyond these three. I am
therefore the secondless, uncontradictable, attributeless Bliss (Siva).   (8)

अपि व्यापकत्वाद्धि तत्त्वप्रयोगात्
    स्वतस्सिद्धभावादनन्याश्रयत्वात् ।
जगत्तुच्छमेतत्समस्तं तदन्यत्
    तदेकोऽवशिष्टः शिवः केवलोऽहम् ॥ ९ ॥

All this universe, being other than the
SELF, is unreal; for the SELF alone is all-
inclusive, constitutes the ultimate goal
and is self-established and self-depen-
dent. I am therefore the secondless, uncontradictable, attributeless Bliss (Siva),
                                          (9)

न चैकं तदन्यद्द्वितीयं कुतःस्यात्
    न वा केवलत्वं न चाकेवलत्वम् ।
न शून्यं न चाशून्यमद्वैतकत्वात्
    कथं सर्ववेदान्तसिद्धं ब्रवीमि ॥ १० ॥

It cannot even be said that It is One.
How then can there be a second, other
than That? There is neither absoluteness nor non-absoluteness, neither non-

entity nor entity; for It is absolutely non-duel in Its nature. How then can I describe That which is established by all the Vedantas?

॥ इति दशश्लोकी समाप्ता ॥

Thus ends the ten-versed hymn.

———

॥ दक्षिणामूर्तिस्तोत्रम् ॥

HYMN TO DAKSHINAMURTI

विश्वं दर्पणदृश्यमाननगरीतुल्यं निजान्तर्गतं
   पश्यन्नात्मनि मायया बहिरिवोद्‌भूतं यथा निद्रया ।
यः साक्षात्कुरुते प्रबोधसमये स्वात्मानमेवाद्वयं
   तस्मै श्रीगुरुमूर्तये नम इदं श्रीदक्षिणामूर्तये ॥ १ ॥

Who, by virtue of the illusion residing
in the self, sees, as in a dream, the
universe as existing outside Himself
although (more truly) it exists within
Himself like the reflection of a city in a
mirror, bnt Who, at the time of the
awakening, sees naught but His own
secondless self,—to that Teacher incarnate, the Lord facing the south, be this
bow.   (1)

बीजस्यान्तरिवाङ्कुरो जगदिदं प्राङ्‌निर्विकल्पं पुनः
   मायाकल्पितदेशकालकलनावैचित्र्यचित्रीकृतम् ।
मायावीव विजृम्भयत्यपि महायोगीव यः स्वेच्छया
   तस्मै श्रीगुरुमूर्तये नम इदं श्रीदक्षिणामूर्तये ॥ २ ॥

Who like a magician or like a *yogi*,
manifests, by His own will, this universe

which at the beginning was undifferentiated like the sprout latent in the seed but
which subsequently became differentiated
under the various conditions of space
and time induced by illusion,—to that
Teacher incarnate, the Lord facing the
south, be this bow.   (2)

यस्यैव स्फुरणं सदात्मकमसत्कल्पार्थकं भासते
  साक्षात्तत्त्वमसीति वेदवचसा यो बोधयत्याश्रितान् ।
यत्साक्षात्करणाद्भवेन्न पुनरावृत्तिर्भवाम्भोनिधौ
  तस्मै श्रीगुरुमूर्तये नम इदं श्रीदक्षिणामूर्तये ॥ ३ ॥

Whose light alone that is the reality
shines in things that resemble non-enti-
ties*; Who directly awakens His devotees by means of the Vedic sentence
" That thou art "; and Who being
realised, there is no more coming back in
this ocean of *Samsara*,—to that Teacher
incarnate, the Lord facing the south, be
this bow.   (3)

---

* Because they have no reality of their own. The
self is the only reality and all else is illusory.

नानाच्छिद्रघटोदरस्थितमहादीपप्रभाभास्वरं
    ज्ञानं यस्य तु चक्षुरादिकरणद्वारा बहि: स्पन्दते ।
जानामीति तमेव भान्तमनुभात्येतत्समस्तं जगत्
    तस्मै श्रीगुरुमूर्तये नम इदं श्रीदक्षिणामूर्तये ॥ ४ ॥

Whose consciousness flows out through
the eye and other senses like the light of
a big lamp placed inside a jar with many
holes, and (thus) this whole universe
shines solely because He shines, namely,
by the consciousness " I know,"—to that
Teacher incarnate, the Lord facing the
south, be this bow.   **(4)**

देहं प्राणमपीन्द्रियाण्यपि चलां बुद्धिं च शून्यं विदुः
    स्त्रीबालान्धजडोपमास्त्वहमिति भ्रान्ता भृशं वादिनः ।
मायाशक्तिविलासकल्पितमहाव्यामोहसंहारिणे
    तस्मै श्रीगुरुमूर्तये नम इदं श्रीदक्षिणामूर्तये ॥ ५ ॥

Deluded persons who talk much, but
who are as ignorant as women and
children, the blind and the stupid, understand, as the " I," the body, or the breath,
or the senses, or the ever-newly-spring-
ing knowledge,* or non-entity. To Him

---

* The reference is to a certain school of Buddhists,

who dispels this great ignorance induced
by the expanslve power of illusion,—to
that Teacher incarnate, the Lord facing
the south, be this bow.   (5)

राहुग्रस्तदिवाकरेन्दुसद्दशो मायासमाच्छादनात्
   सन्मात्रः करणोपसंहरणतो योऽभूत्सुषुप्तः पुमान् ।
श्रागस्वाप्समिति प्रबोधसमये यः प्रत्यभिज्ञायते
   तस्मै श्रीगुरुमूर्तये नम इदं श्रीदक्षिणामूर्तये ॥ ६ ॥

Who is the inner self which, under the
veil of illusion, like the sun or the moon
eclipsed, merely exists † in deep sleep
owing to the withdrawal of the senses, but,
which one when He wakes, is recognised
by Him as "I have slept,"—to that
Teacher incarnate, the Lord facing the
south, be this bow.   (6)

बाल्यादिष्वपि जाग्रदादिषु तथा सर्वास्ववस्थास्वपि
   व्यावृत्तास्खनुवर्तेमानमहमित्यन्तस्फुरन्तं तदा ।
स्वात्मानं प्रकटीकरोति भजतां यो मुद्रया भद्रया
   तस्मै श्रीगुरुमूर्तये नम इदं दक्षिणामूर्तये ॥ ७ ॥

---

* Maya.   † Since knowledge is latent in sleep.

Who reveals to His devotees, by
means of the blessed symbol, * His own
self which, for ever, shines within as the
" I ", unchanging through all the chang-
ing states of childhood, youth and old
age, waking, dream and sleep, etc.,—to
that Teacher incarnate, the Lord facing
the south, be this bow.   (7)

विश्वं पश्यति कार्यकारणतया स्वस्वामिसम्बन्धतः
शिष्याचार्यतया तथैव पितृपुत्राद्यात्मना भेदतः ।
स्वप्ने जाग्रति वा य एष पुरुषो मायापरिभ्रामितः
तस्मै श्रीगुरुमूर्तये नम इदं श्रीदक्षिणामूर्तये ॥ ८ ॥

Who is the supreme self that, dreaming
or waking, under the sway of illusion,
sees the universe under various distinctions such as that of cause and effect,
owner and owned, pupil and teacher,
father and son,—to that Teacher incarnate, the Lord facing the south, be this
bow.   (8)

---

* The *jnana-mudra*, in which the thumb and the
fore-finger are formed into a ring.

भूरम्भांस्यनलोऽनिलोऽम्बरमहर्नाथो हिमांशुः पुमान्
　इत्याभाति चराचरात्मकमिदं यस्यैव मूर्त्यष्टकम् ।
नान्यत्किञ्चन विद्यते विमृशतां यस्मात्परस्माद्विभोः
　तस्मै श्रीगुरुमूर्तये नम इदं श्रीदक्षिणामूर्तये ॥९॥

Whose eight-fold form alone, namely,
earth, water, fire, air, ether, sun, moon and
soul, manifests itself as this sentiment
and non-sentient universe; than Whom
supreme and infinite naught else is perceived by the seekers of reality,—to that
Teacher incarnate, the Lord facing the
south, be this bow. (9)

सर्वात्मत्वमिति स्फुटीकृतमिदं यस्मादमुष्मिन्स्तवे
　तेनास्य श्रवणात्तदर्थमननाद्ध्यानाच्च सङ्कीर्तनात् ।
सर्वात्मत्वमहाविभूतिसहितं स्यादीश्वरत्वं स्वतः
　सिध्येत्तत्पुनरष्टधा परिणतं चैश्वर्यमव्याहतम् ॥१०॥

Since, in this hymn, the identity of the
self with the universe has been made
clear, by listening to it, by understanding
its meaning, by meditating on it, and by
teaching it to others, one will acquire the
supreme faculty of identity with the

universe, together with the overlordship
of nature and the eight-fold divine
faculty. *   (10)

|| इति दक्षिणामूर्तिस्तोत्रं संम्पूर्णम् ||

Thus ends the hymn to Dakshinamurti.

-----

* अणिमा, महिमा, गरिमा, लघिमा, प्राप्तिः, प्राकाम्यं,
ईशित्वं, वशित्वम्.

॥ अपरोक्षानुभूतिः ॥

DIRECT REALISATION

श्रीहरिं परमानन्दमुपदेष्टारमीश्वरम् ।
व्यापकं सर्वलोकानां कारणं तं नमाम्यहम् ॥ १ ॥

I bow to that Sri Hari (Vishnu), the infinite bliss, the Teacher, the Supreme
Lord, all-pervading, the prime-cause of
all the worlds.   (1)

अपरोक्षानुभूतिर्वै प्रोच्यते मोक्षसिद्धये ।
सद्भिरेव प्रयत्नेन वीक्षणीया मुहुर्मुहुः ॥ २ ॥

Direct realisation is herein expounded
as a means to liberation. It should be
studied, again and again, with great
effort, only by the wise.   (2)

स्ववर्णाश्रमधर्मेण तपसा हरितोषणात् ।
साधनं प्रभवेत्पुंसां वैराग्यादिचतुष्टयम् ॥ ३ ॥

By following the duties of one's own
caste and order, by asceticism and by the
propitiation of Hari, men will gain the
four-fold requisite of freedom from
desires, etc.   (3)

ब्रह्मादिस्थावरान्तेषु वैराग्यं विषयेष्वनु ।
यथैव काकविष्ठाया वैराग्यं तद्धि निर्मलम् ॥ ४ ॥

Spotless freedom from desires means
such a dissatisfaction in respect of all
objects from Brahman down to the inanimate as is felt in respect of the excrement
of a crow.   (4)

नित्यमात्मस्वरूपं हि दृश्यं तद्विपरीतगम् ।
एवं यो निश्चयः सम्यग्विवेको वस्तुनः स वै ॥ ५ ॥

Discrimination of the real means the
determination that the nature of the self
is eternal while all that is perceptible is
otherwise.   (5)

सदैव वासनात्यागः शमोऽयमिति शब्दितः ।
निग्रहो बाह्यवृत्तीनां दम इत्यभिधीयते ॥ ६ ॥

The constant eradication of mental
impressions is called control of mind.
The restraint of external activities is
called control of body.   (6)

विषयेभ्यः परावृत्तिः परमोपरतिर्हि सा ।
सहनं सर्वदुःखानां तितिक्षा सा शुभा मता ॥ ७ ॥

Extreme abstention is the turning away from the objects of enjoyment. The endurance of all kinds of pain is called resignation, which is beneficial.   (7)

निगमाचार्यवाक्येषु भक्तिः श्रद्धेति विश्रुता ।

चित्तैकाग्र्यं तु सल्लक्ष्ये समाधानमिति स्मृतम् ॥८॥

Devoted belief in the saying of the Vedas, and of the teacher is called faith. The concentration of the mind on the reality that is the ultimate goal is called balance.   (8)

संसारबन्धनिर्मुक्तिः कथं मे स्यात्कदा विभो ।

इति या सुदृढा बुद्धिर्वक्तव्या सा मुमुक्षुता ॥ ९ ॥

Desire for liberation is the name given to the intense thought "How and when, O Lord, shall liberation from the bonds of *Samsara* come to me?"   (9)

उक्तसाधनयुक्तेन विचारः पुरुषेण हि ।

कर्तव्या ज्ञानसिद्ध्यर्थमात्मनः शुभमिच्छता ॥१०॥

Whosoever desires his own welfare should, after acquiring the above mentioned qualifications, commence the enquiry with a view to the attainment of knowledge. (10)

नोत्पद्यते विना ज्ञानं विचारेणान्यसाधनैः ।
स्था पदार्थभानं हि प्रकाशेन विना कचित् ॥ ११ ॥

Knowledge cannot spring up by any other means than enquiry, just as the preception of things is impossible without light. (11)

कोऽहं कथमिदं जातं को वा कर्तास्य विद्यते ।
उपादानं किमस्तीह विचारः सोऽयमीदृशः ॥ १२ ॥

"Who am I? How was this (universe) born? Who is its Maker? What is its material cause?" This is the kind of enquiry referred to above. (12)

नाहं भूतगणो देहो नाहं चाक्षगणस्तथा ।
एतद्विलक्षणः कश्चिद्विचारः सोऽयमीदृशः ॥ १३ ॥

"I am not the body which is a mere conglomeration of the elements, nor am I the group of the senses, but am something different from all these." This is the kind of enquiry referred to above. (13)

अज्ञानप्रभवं सर्वं ज्ञानेन प्रविलीयते ।
सङ्कल्पो विविधः कर्ता विचारः सोऽयमीदृशः ॥ १४ ॥

"All this (universe) has its origin in
ignorance and is dissolved by knowledge,
Desire, in its various aspects, is the
mainspring of all action." This is the
kind of enquiry referred to above.   (14)

एतयोर्येदुपादानमेकं सूक्ष्मं सदव्ययम् ।
यथैव मृद्घटादीनां विचारः सोऽयमीदृशः ॥ १५ ॥

"The prime cause of both these (viz.,
ignorance and desire) is the one, subtle
and immutable Reality, even as the clay
is the prime cause of the earthen vessel
etc." This is the kind of enquiry referred
to above.   (15)

अहमेकोऽपि सूक्ष्मश्च ज्ञाता साक्षी सदव्ययः ।
तदहं नात्र सन्देहो विचारः सोऽयमीदृशः ॥ १६ ॥

"I too am the one, subtle, and immutable Reality, the knower, the witness.
I am That, without doubt." This is the
kind of enquiry referred to above.   (16)

---

* Brahman.

आत्मा विनिष्कलो ह्येको देहो बहुभिरावृतः ।
तयोरैक्यं प्रपश्यन्ति किमज्ञानमतः परम् ॥ १७ ॥

The self is without parts and without a
second; but the body is comprised of
many parts. And yet they identify the
two. Can any ignorance be worse than
this?   (17)

आत्मा नियामकश्चान्तर्देहो बाह्यो नियाम्यकः ।
तयोरैक्यं प्रपश्यन्ति किमज्ञानमतः परम् ॥ १८ ॥

The self is the ruler and subjective; the
body is the ruled and objective. And yet
they identify the two. Can any ignorance be worse than this?   (18)

आत्मा ज्ञानमयः पुण्यो देहो मांसमयोऽशुचिः ।
तयोरैक्यं प्रपश्यन्ति किमज्ञानमतः परम् ॥ १९ ॥

The self is of the nature of knowledge
and pure; the body consists of flesh and
is impure. And yet they identify the
two. Can any ignorance be worse than
this?   (19)

आत्मा प्रकाशकः स्वच्छो देहस्तामस उच्यते ।
तयोरैक्यं प्रपश्यन्ति किमज्ञानमतः परम् ॥ २० ॥

The self is that which illuminates and is absolutely pure; the body is inert.* And yet they identify the two. Can any ignorance be worse than this?   (20)

आत्मा नित्यो हि सद्रूपो देहोऽनित्यो ह्यसन्मयः ।
तयोरैक्यं प्रपश्यन्ति किमज्ञानमतः परम् ॥ २१ ॥

The self is eternal and real by nature; the body is transient and unreal. And yet they identify the two. Can any ignorance be worse than this?   (21)

आत्मनस्तत्प्रकाशत्वं यत्पदार्थोवभासनम् ।
नाग्न्यादिदीप्तिवद्दीप्तिर्भवत्यान्ध्यं यतो निशि ॥२२॥

The resplendence of the self consists in its making all things cognisable. Its shining is not like that of fire etc., for there is darkness at night (in spite of their presence in one place),   (22)

देहोऽहमियियं मूढः कृत्वा तिष्ठत्यहो जनः ।
ममायमित्यपि ज्ञात्वा घटद्रष्टेव सर्वदा ॥ २३ ॥

---

* That which is illuminated.

He who thinks "I am the body"
remains, alas in ignorance, as also he
who thinks "this body is mine," as if he
were always looking at an earthen vessel
belonging to him.   (23)

ब्रह्मैवाहं समः शान्तः सच्चिदानन्दलक्षणः ।

नाहं देहो ह्यसद्रूपो ज्ञानमित्युच्यते बुधैः ॥ २४ ॥

"I am indeed Brahman, without difference, without change, and of the nature
of reality, knowledge and bliss. I am not,
therefore, the body which is unreal."
This is what the wise call knowledge. (24)

निर्विकारो निराकारो निरवद्योऽहमव्ययः ।

नाहं देहो ह्यसद्रूपो ज्ञानमित्युच्यते बुधैः ॥ २५ ॥

"I am without change, without form,
without blemish and without decay. I am
not, therefore, the body which is unreal."
This is what the wise call knowledge. (25)

निरामयो निराभासो निर्विकल्पोऽहमाततः ।

नाहं देहो ह्यसद्रूपो ज्ञानमित्युच्यते बुधैः ॥ २६ ॥

"I am without disease, without ap-
pearances, without alternatives, and

all-prevading. I am not, therefore, the
body which is unreal." This is what the
wise call knowledge.   (26)

निर्गुणो निष्क्रियो नित्यो निलमुक्तोऽहमच्युतः ।
नाहं देहो ह्मसद्रूपो ज्ञानमित्युच्यते बुधैः ॥ २७ ॥

"I am without attribute, without action,
eternal, eternally free, and imperishable.
I am not, therefore, the body which is
unreal." This is what the wise call
knowledge.   (27)

निर्मलो निश्चलोऽनन्तः शुद्धोऽहमजरोऽमरः ।
नाहं देहो ह्मसद्रूपो ज्ञानमित्युच्यते बुधैः ॥ २८ ॥

"I am stainless, without motion, without end, pure, and devoid of old age and
death. I am not, therefore, the body
which is unreal." This is what the wise
call knowledge.   (28)

खदेहे शोभनं सन्तं पुरुषार्ख्यं च सम्मतम् ।
किं मूर्ख शून्यमात्मानं देहातीतं करोषि भो ॥ २९ ॥

Why, fool, dost thou imagine to be an
absolute void the self which is different
from the body but which resides even in

your body as the informing spirit * auspicious, real, accepted by all?   (29)

स्वात्मानं श्रृणु मूर्खे त्वं श्रुत्या युक्त्या च पूरुषम् ।
देहातीतं सदाकारं सुदुर्दर्शं भवादृशैः ॥ ३० ॥

Fool, learn from the Veda and by
reasoning the nature of the own self
which is the informing spirit beyond the
body, absolutely real by nature and
utterly incomprehensible by men like
you.   (30)

अहंशब्देन विख्यात एक एव स्थितः परः ।
स्थूलस्त्वनेकतां प्राप्तः कथं स्यादेहकः पुमान् ॥३१॥

That which is denoted by the word
"I" forever remains sole and transcendental. That which is gross, on the
other hand, undergoes multiplicity. How
then can the body be the self?   (31)

अहं द्रष्ट्टतया सिद्धो देहो दृश्यतया स्थितः ।
ममायमिति निर्देशात्कथं स्यादेहकः पुमान् ॥३२॥

The "I" is assuredly the preceiver
and the body the perceived, as is evident
from the expression "this body is mine."
How then can the body be the self?   (32)

* Purusha.

अहं विकारहीनस्तु देहो नित्यं विकारवान् ।
इति प्रतीयते साक्षात्कथं स्यादेहकः पुमान् ॥ ३३ ॥

It is a matter of direct experience that
the "I" is devoid of change, whereas
the body is undergoing incessant change.
How then can the body be the self? (33)

यस्मात्परमिति श्रुत्या तया पुरुषलक्षणम् ।
विनिर्णीतं विमूढेन कथं स्यादेहकः पुमान् ॥ ३४ ॥

The wise have ascertained the exact
nature of the self from the Vedic passage
"Than whom there is naught higher,
etc."* How then can the body be the
self? (34)

सर्वं पुरुष एवेति सूक्ते पुरुषसंज्ञिते ।
अप्युच्यते यतः श्रुत्यां कथं स्यादेहकः पुमान् ॥३५॥

It is further declared by the Veda in
the *Purusha-sukta* that all this universe is
verily the self. How then can the body
be the self? (35)

असङ्गः पुरुषः प्रोक्तो बृहदारण्यकेऽपि च ।
अनन्तमलसंश्लिष्टः कथं स्यादेहकः पुमान् ॥३६॥

---

*"Than whom there is naught else that is higher
naught that is smaller or bigger. It stands in space
unmoving, like a tree. By that, which is the Self all
this universe is filled."

Further, it is declared in the *Brihadar-nyaka Upanishad* that the self is inconta-minable. How then can the body, con-taminated by numberless impurities, be the self. (36)

तत्रैव च समाख्यातस्वयंज्योतिर्हि पूरुषः ।

जडः परप्रकाश्योऽसौ कथं स्यादेहकः पुमान् ॥३७॥

In that same *Upanishad* it is declared that the self is indeed self-resplendent. How then can the body, inert and requir-ing to be illuminated by another, be the self ? (37)

प्रोक्तोऽपि कर्मकाण्डेन ह्यात्मा देहाद्विलक्षणः ।

नित्यश्च तत्फलं भुङ्क्ते देहपातादनन्तरम् ॥ ३८ ॥

Even the ritual portion of the Veda declares that the self, distinct from the body and eternal, enjoys the fruits of ritual after the demise of the body. (38)

लिङ्गं चानेकसंयुक्तं चलं दृश्यं विकारि च ।

अव्यापकमसद्रूपं तत्कथं स्यात्पुमानयम् ॥ ३९ ॥

Even the subtle body*, composed of many parts, unstable, objective, mutable, finite, and unreal,—how can it be the self ? (39)

---

*Linga-sarira.

एवं देहद्वयादन्य आत्मा पुरुष ईश्वरः ।
सर्वात्मा सर्वरूपश्च सर्वातीतोऽहमव्ययः ॥ ४० ॥

The self is thus distinct from both the
gross and the subtle bodies. It is the
informing Spirit, the Supreme Lord, the
soul of all, identical with all, beyond all ,
the "I", the immutable. (40)

इत्यात्मदेहभागेन प्रपञ्चस्यैव सत्यता ।
यथोक्ता तर्कशास्त्रेण ततः किं पुरुषार्थता ॥ ४१ ॥

(Says the opponent.) By the above-
distinction between the self and the
body, it only follows that the manifested
world is real, as declared by the science
of logic. † Your aim therefore fails. (41)

इत्यात्मदेहभेदेन देहात्मत्वं निवारितम् ।
इदानीं देहभेदस्य ह्यसत्त्वं स्फुटमुच्यते ॥ ४२ ॥

(This is the answer.) By the above distinction between the self and the body,
the identification of the body with the
self has alone been refuted. The unreality of the body as a separate entity will
now be clearly explained. (42)

---

† Tarka-sastra.

चैतन्यस्यैकरूपत्वाद्भेदो युक्तो न कर्हिंचित् ।
जीवत्वं च मृषा ज्ञेयं रज्जौ सर्पग्रहो यथा ॥ ४३ ॥

Since consciousness is one by nature,
no distinction is admissible under any
circumstances. Even the condition of the
individual soul must be understood to be
unreal like the apprehension of a serpent
in a rope. (43)

रज्जवज्ञानात्क्षणेनैव यद्वद्रज्जुर्हि सर्पिणी ।
भाति तद्वच्चितिः साक्षाद्विश्वाकारेण केवला ॥४४॥

As the rope, in consequence of one's
ignorance of it, appears in an instant as a
serpent, so does consciousness, which is
ever pure, manifest itself as the universe.
 (44)

उपादानं प्रपञ्चस्य ब्रह्मणोऽन्यन्न विद्यते ।
तस्मात्सर्वप्रपञ्चोऽयं ब्रह्मैवास्ति न चेतरत् ॥ ४५ ॥

There can be no other material cause of
the universe than *Brahman.* All this universe, therefore, is only *Brahman* and
naught else. (45)

व्याप्यव्यापकता मिथ्या सर्वमात्मेति शासनात् ।
इति ज्ञाते परे तत्त्वे भेदस्यावसरः कुतः ॥ ४६ ॥

The distinction of the pervader and
the pervaded is unreal by reason of the
declaration "The self is all." If the
highest truth is thus understood, how can
there be room for difference?   (46)

श्रुत्या निवारितं नूनं नानात्वं स्वमुखेन हि ।
कथं भासो भवेदन्यः स्थिते चाद्वयकारणे ॥ ४७ ॥

Indeed, multiplicity is directly contra-
dicted by the Veda.* How can there be
any manifestation different from the one
(secondless) cause?   (47)

दोषोऽपि विहितः श्रुत्या मृत्योर्मृत्युं स गच्छति ।
इह पश्यति नानात्वं मायया वञ्चितो नरः ॥ ४८ ॥

The Veda has also pointed out the evil
consequence, namely, that the man who,
duped by illusion, perceives multiplicity
in this world, passes on from death to
death. †   (48)

ब्रह्मणः सर्वभूतानि जायन्ते परमात्मनः ।
तस्मादेतानि ब्रह्मैव भवन्तीत्यवधारयेत् ॥ ४९ ॥

---

* नेह नानाऽस्ति किञ्चन *i. e.* there is naught of
multiplicity in this word.

† *i.e.* Is born again and again : does not become free.

All creatures are born of Brahman, the Supreme Self. One should therefore understand that all these are Brahman itself.   (49)

ब्रह्मैव सर्वनामानि रूपाणि विविधानि च ।

कर्माण्यपि समग्राणि बिभर्तीति श्रुतिर्जगौ ॥ ५० ॥

The Veda has declared that Brahman alone assumes all names, all forms and all activities.   (50)

सुवर्णाज्जायमानस्य सुवर्णत्वं च शाश्वतम् ।

ब्रह्मणो जायमानस्य ब्रह्मत्वं च तथा भवेत् ॥५१॥

Whatever is made of gold retains for ever the nature of gold. So, too, all that is born of Brahman is of the nature of Brahman.   (51)

स्वल्पमप्यन्तरं कृत्वा जीवात्मपरमात्मनोः ।

यस्संतिष्ठति मूढात्मा भयं तस्याभिभाषितम् ॥५२॥

The Veda has declared that the ignorant man who rests content with making the slightest distinction between the individual soul and the Supreme Self is exposed to danger.   (52)

यत्राज्ञानाद्वेद्द्वैतमितरस्तत्र पश्यति ।
आत्मत्वेन यदा सर्वं नेतरस्तत्र चाण्वपि ॥ ५३ ॥

Where there is duality by virtue of
ignorance one sees all things as distinct
from the self.   When everything is seen
as the self, then there is not even an
atom other than the self.   (53)

यस्मिन्सर्वाणि भूतानि ह्यात्मत्वेन विजानतः ।
न वै तस्य भवेन्मोहो न च शोकोऽद्वितीयतः ॥५४॥

For him who has realised that all
beings are the self, there is neither delusion nor misery, since there is no second,
                                      (54)

अयमात्मा हि ब्रह्मैव सर्वात्मकतया स्थितः ।
इति निर्धारितं श्रुत्या बृहदारण्यसंस्थया ॥ ५५ ॥

It has been established in a passage of
the Brihadaranyaka that this self is
Brahman itself which is everything. (55)

अनुभूतोऽप्ययं लोको व्यवहारक्षमोऽपि सन् ।
असद्रूपो यथा स्वप्न उत्तरक्षणबाधतः ॥ ५६ ॥

This world, although it is the object of
experience   and   of   phenomenal   treat-

ment, is yet unreal like a dream, because
it is followed by contradiction.*   (56)

स्वप्रो जागरणेऽलीकः स्वप्रेऽपि न हि जागरः ।
द्वयमेव लये नास्ति लयोऽपि ह्युभयोर्न च ॥ ५७ ॥

A dream, becomes unreal in the waking
state ; nor does the waking state exist in
dream. Both dream and waking are
absent in sleep, and sleep too is absent
in dream and in waking.   (57)

त्रयमेव भवेन्मिथ्या गुणत्रयविनिर्मितम् ।
अस्य द्रष्टा गुणातीतो नित्यो ह्येकश्चिदात्मकः ॥

Thus all the three states are unreal,
being produced by the three qualities.†
The Eternal is the witness of these three
states, beyond the three qualities, the
One that is pure consciousness.   (58)

यद्वन्मृदि घटभ्रान्ति शुक्तौ वा रजतस्थितिम् ।
तद्वद्ब्रह्मणि जीवत्वं वीक्ष्यमाणे न पश्यति॥५९॥

Just as one sees not the separate existence of the pot when he knows that it is

---

* Whcn Brahman is realised.

† *Sattva*, *rajas* and *tamas*.

clay, or the illusive existence of silver
when he knows that it is mother-of-pearl,
so too does one see not the condition of
the individual soul when he knows
Brahman.   (59)

यथा मृदि घटीनाम कनके कुण्डलाभिधा ।
शुक्तौ हि रजतख्यातिर्जीवशब्दस्तथा परे ॥ ६० ॥

Just as a pot is only a name of clay, an
ear-ring of gold, or the (illusive) silver of
mother-of-pearl, so too is the individual
soul a name of the supreme.   (60)

यथैव व्योम्नि नीलत्वं यथा नीरं मरुस्थले ।
पुरुषत्वं यथा स्थाणौ तद्वद्विश्वं चिदात्मनि ॥ ६१ ॥

Like the blueness in the sky, like the
mirage in the desert and like the illusive
appearance of a person in a post, so is
the universe in Brahman.   (61)

यथैव शून्ये वेतालो गन्धर्वाणां पुरं यथा ।
यथाऽऽकाशे द्विचन्द्रत्वं तद्वत्सत्ये जगत्स्थिति: ॥

Like a ghost in vacant space, like a
city of the celestials* and like two moons

---

*An accidental formation of the clouds resembling
a city.

in the sky, so is the existence of the
world in Brahman.   (62)

यथा तरङ्गकल्लोलैर्जलमेव स्फुरत्यलम् ।
पात्ररूपेण ताम्रं हि ब्रह्माण्डौघैस्तथाऽऽत्मता ॥

Just as it is water alone that appears as
waves and tides, and copper alone as ves-
sels, so does the self alone appear as
many universes.   (63)

घटनाम्ना यथा पृथ्वी पटनाम्ना हि तन्तवः ।
जगन्नाम्ना चिदाभाति ज्ञेयं तत्तदभावतः ॥ ६४ ॥

As the clay alone appears under the
name of pot, as the threads appear under
the name of cloth, so does Brahman
appear under the name of the world. It
(Brahman) should therefore, be realised
by the elimination of name.   (64)

सर्वोऽपि व्यवहारस्तु ब्रह्मणा क्रियते जनैः ।
अज्ञानान्न विजानन्ति मृदेव हि घटादिकम् ॥ ६५ ॥

All phenomenal life is possible for men
only by virtue of Brahman, just as the pot

is possible only by virtue of clay. But
men do not understand it thus, owing to
ignorance. (65)

कार्यकारणता नियमास्ते घटमृदोर्येथा ।
तथैव श्रुतियुक्तिभ्यां प्रपञ्चब्रह्मणोरिह ॥ ६६ ॥

Just as the relation of effect and cause
always subsists between the pot and clay,
so does the same relation subsist between
the world and Brahman. This is known
both from the Vedas and by reasoning.
(66)

गृह्यमाणे घटे यद्वन्मृत्तिकाऽऽयाति वै बलात् ।
वीक्ष्यमाणे प्रपञ्चेऽपि ब्रह्मैवाभाति भासुरम् ॥६७॥

Just as, when the pot is being seen, it
is the clay that is seen *ipso facto*, so too
when the world is being seen, it is only
the self-resplendent Brahman this is seen.
(67)

सदैवात्मा विशुद्धोऽस्ति ह्यशुद्धो भाति वै सदा ।
यथैव द्विविधा रज्जुज्ञानिनोऽज्ञानिनोऽनिशम् ॥

The self always shines as unconditioned for the wise and always as condi-

tioned for the ignorant, just as the rope
appears in two ways.*   (68)

यथैव मृण्मयः कुम्भस्तद्वद्देहोऽपि चिन्मयः ।
आत्मानात्मविभागोऽयं मुधैव क्रियते बुधैः ॥ ६९ ॥

Just as the pot consists of clay, so does
even the body consist of the self. This
distinction between the self and the not-
self is therefore unnecessary for the wise.
                                             (69)

सर्पत्वेन यथा रज्जू रजतत्वेन शुक्तिका ।
विनिर्णीता विमूढेन देहत्वेन तथाऽऽत्मता ॥ ७० ॥

As a rope is perceived as a serpent, or
the mother-of-pearl as silver, so too is the
self understood as the body by the
utterly ignorant.   (70)

घटत्वेन यथा पृथ्वी पटत्वेनैव तन्तवः ।
विनिर्णीता विमूढेन देहत्वेन तथाऽऽत्मता ॥ ७१ ॥

As clay is perceived as a pot, as
threads are perceived as a cloth, so too

---

*As a rope to the clear vision or as a serpent to the
mistaken vision.

is the self understood as the body by the
utterly ignorant.   (71)

कनकं कुण्डलत्वेन तरङ्गत्वेन वै जलम् ।
विनिर्णीता विमूढेन देहत्वेन तथाऽऽत्मता ॥७२॥

As gold is perceived as an ear-ring or
water as a wave, so too is the self understood as the body by the utterly ignorant.   (72)

चोरत्वेन यथा स्थाणुर्जलत्वेन मरीचिका ।
विनिर्णीता विमूढेन देहत्वेन तथाऽऽत्मता ॥७३॥

As a post is perceived as a thief or the
mirage as water, so too is the self understood as the body by the utterly ignorant.   (73)

गृहत्वेनेव काष्ठानि खड्गत्वेनेव लोहता ।
विनिर्णीता विमूढेन देहत्वेन तथाऽऽत्मता ॥७४॥

As pieces of wood are perceived as a
house or as a steel is perceived as a
sword, so too is the self understood as the
body by the utterly ignorant.   (74)

यथा वृक्षविपर्यासो जलाद्भवति कस्यचित् ।
तद्वदात्मनि देहत्वं पश्यत्यज्ञानयोगतः ॥ ७५ ॥

Just as trees are seen by one as topsy-
turvy by reflection in water, so does one
perceive the self as the body by virtue of
ignorance.   (75)

पोतेन गच्छतः पुंसः सर्वं भातीव चञ्चलम् ॥
तद्वदात्मनि देहत्वं पश्यत्यज्ञानयोगतः ॥ ७६ ॥

For the person who is going in a boat,
everything appears to be in motion, so
does one perceive the self as the body by
virtue of ignorance.   (76)

पीतत्वं हि यथा शुभ्रे दोषाद्भवति कस्यचित् ।
तद्वदात्मनि देहत्वं पश्यत्यज्ञानयोगतः ॥ ७७ ॥

Just as some one with a faulty vision
sees a white thing as yellow, so does one
perceive the self as the body by virtue of
ignorance.   (77)

चक्षुर्भ्यां भ्रमशीलाभ्यां सर्वं भाति भ्रमात्मकम् ।
तद्वदात्मनि देहत्वं पश्यत्यज्ञानयोगतः ॥ ७८ ॥

Just as, when the eyes are dizzy, everything appears as wandering, so does one
perceive the self as the body by virtue of
ignorance.   (78)

अलातं भ्रमणेनैव वर्तुलं भाति सूर्यवत् ।
तद्वदात्मनि देहत्वं पश्यत्यज्ञानयोगतः ॥ ७९ ॥

Just as a firebrand, by being revolved,
appears to be circular like the sun, so
does one perceive the self as the body by
virtue of ignorance.   (79)

महत्त्वे सर्ववस्तूनामणुत्वं ह्यतिदूरतः ।
तद्वदात्मनि देहत्वं पश्यत्यज्ञानयोगतः ॥८०॥

All things, however big in size, appear
very small at a great distance. So does
one perceive the self as the body by
virtue of ignorance.   (80)

सूक्ष्मत्वे सर्वभावानां स्थूलत्वं चोपनेत्रतः ।
तद्वदात्मनि देहत्वं पश्यत्यज्ञानयोगतः ॥ ८१ ॥

All things, however small in size,
appear big under a magnifying glass. So

does one perceive the self as the body by
virtue of ignorance.   (81)

काचभूमौ जलत्वं वा जलभूमौ हि काचता ।
तद्वदात्मनि देहत्वं पश्यत्यज्ञानयोगतः ॥ ८२ ॥

A glassy surface appears as water, and
a watery surface as glass. So does one
perceive the self as the body by virtue of
ignorance.   (82)

यद्वदग्नौ मणित्वं हि मणौ वा वह्निता पुमान् ।
तद्वदात्मनि देहत्वं पश्यत्यज्ञानयोगतः ॥ ८३ ॥

Just as one mistakes charcoal for a gem
or a gem for charcoal, so does one perceive the self as the body by virtue of
ignorance.   (83)

अभ्रेषु सत्सु धावत्सु सोमो धावति भाति वै ।
तद्वदात्मनि देहत्वं पश्यत्यज्ञानयोगतः ॥ ८४ ॥

When the clouds are moving, the
moon appears to move. So does one perceive the self as the body by virtue of
ignorance.   (84)

यथैव दिग्विपर्यासो मोहाद्भवति कस्यचित् ।
तद्वदात्मनि देहत्वं पश्यत्यज्ञानयोगतः ॥ ८५ ॥

Just as the directions seem to be
changed for one who is in a swoon, so
does one perceive the self as the body by
virtue of ignorance.   (85)

यथा शशी जले भाति चञ्चलत्वेन कस्यचित् ।
तद्वदात्मनि देहत्वं पश्यत्यज्ञानयोगतः ॥ ८६ ॥

Just as the moon appears to some one
as moving in the waters, so does one
perceive the self as the body by virtue of
ignorance.   (86)

एवमात्मन्यविद्यातो देहाध्यासो हि जायते ।
स एवात्मपरिज्ञानाल्लीयते च परात्मनि ॥ ८७ ॥

Thus is the self mistaken for the body
owing to ignorance. But when the self is
realised, this mistake disappears in Brahman.   (87)

सर्वमात्मतया ज्ञातं जगत्स्थावरजङ्गमम् ।
अभावात्सर्वभावानां देहानां चात्मता कुतः ॥८८॥

The whole world, sentient and non-
sentient, is realised to be only the self.

How then can the various things and the various bodies be the self, since they are unreal?   (88)

आत्मानं सततं जानन् कालं नय महामते ।
प्रारब्धमखिलं भुञ्जन्नोद्वेगं कर्तुमर्हसि ॥ ८९ ॥

O thou that art most intelligent! Spend all thy time in realising the self. Exhausting all the ripe fruits of thy past deeds, thou needest not feel any anxiety. (89)

उत्पन्नेऽप्यात्मनि ज्ञाने प्रारब्धं नैव मुञ्चति ।
इति यच्छ्रूयते शास्त्रे तन्निराक्रियतेऽधुना ॥ ९० ॥

We shall now refute the statement in the books that, even when the self has been realised, such fruits of past actions as are ripe for experience cannot be avoided.   (90)

तत्त्वज्ञानोदयादूर्ध्वं प्रारब्धं नैव विद्यते ।
देहादीनामसत्त्वात्तु यथा स्वप्नो विबोधतः ॥ ९१ ॥

When the knowledge of the reality has sprung up, there can be no fruits of· past

---

* Prarabdha.

actions to be experienced, owing to the
unreality of the body, etc., in the same
way as there can be no dream after
waking.   (91)

कर्म जन्मान्तरीयं यत्प्रारब्धमिति कीर्तितम् ।

तत्तु जन्मान्तराभावात्पुंसो नैवास्ति कर्हिचित् ॥९२॥

Action done in past lives is called
prarabdha. But that has no existence at
all at any time. since past life is itself
unreal.   (92)

स्वप्नदेहो यथाऽध्यस्तस्तथैवायं हि देहकः ।

अध्यस्तस्य कुतो जन्म जन्माभावे हि तत्कुतः ॥

Just as the dream body is a mere
illusion, so is this (physical) body also.
How can an illusory thing have life, and
how, if there is no life, can there be that
(past action) ?   (93)

उपादानं प्रपञ्चस्य मृद्घटाण्डस्येव कथ्यते ।

अज्ञानं चैव वेदान्तैस्तस्मिन्नष्टे क विश्वता ॥ ९४ ॥

As clay is the efficient cause of the pot,
so is ignorance declared by the Vedanta
to be the efficient cause of the universe.

When that ignorance itself is destroyed,
where then is this universe ?   (94)

यथा रज्जुं परित्यज्य सर्पं गृह्णाति वै भ्रमात् ।
तद्वत्सत्यमविज्ञाय जगत्पश्यति मूढधीः ॥ ९५ ॥

Just as, by delusion, one ignores the
rope and preceives the serpent, so does
he of deluded intellect perceive the
universe without realising the truth.   (95)

रज्जुरूपे परिज्ञाते सर्पखण्डं न तिष्ठति ।
अधिष्ठाने तथा ज्ञाते प्रपञ्चः शून्यतां गतः ॥ ९६ ॥

When the form of the rope is understood, the appearance of a serpent disappears. So too when the ultimate
reality is realised, the universe vanishes.
                                        (96)

देहस्यापि प्रपञ्चत्वात्प्रारब्धावस्थितिः कुतः ।
अज्ञानिजनबोधार्थं प्रारब्धं वक्ति वै श्रुतिः ॥ ९७ ॥

And as the body too is part of the universe, how can any past action subsist ?
But the Vedas speak of past action in
order to help the understanding of the
ignorant.   (97)

क्षीयन्ते चास्य कर्माणि तस्मिन्दृष्टे परावरे ।

बहुत्वं तन्निषेधार्थं श्रुत्या गीतं च यत्स्फुटम् ॥९८॥

In the passage "his actions are
destroyed when the supreme is realised",
the Veda expressly speaks of actions in
the plural, in order to signify the
destruction of *prarabdha*   (98)

उच्यतेऽज्ञैर्बलाच्चैत्तदाऽनर्थद्वयागमः ।

वेदान्तमतहानं च यतो ज्ञानमिति श्रुतिः ॥ ९९ ॥

There is a twofold fault † in the obsti-
nate insistence on *prarabdha* by the
ignorant. There is also the forsaking of
the Vedanta doctrine, since the Veda
declares the possibility of knowledge. (99)

---

*There are three kinds of actions :—(1) *prarabdha*
so much of past actions as has given rise to the
present birth, (2) *sanchita*, the balance of past actions
that will give rise to future births and (3) *kriyamana*,
acts being done in the present life. If by knowledge,
(2) and (3) were alone to be destroyed and not (1) also,
the dual number would have been used and not the
plural.

† The impossibility of liberation and the futility of
knowledge.

त्रिपञ्चाङ्गान्यथो वक्ष्ये पूर्वोक्तस्य हि लब्धये ।
तैश्च सर्वेंस्सदा कार्यं निदिध्यासनमेव तु ॥ १०० ॥

For the gaining of the liberation aforesaid, I shall now explain fifteen steps, by
the help of all of which one should at all
times practice meditation.   (100)

नित्याभ्यासाद्दते प्राप्तिन भवेत्सच्चिदात्मनः ।
तस्माद्ब्रह्म निदिध्यासेज्जिज्ञासुः श्रेयसे चिरम् ॥

Without constant practice the self that
is pure existence and knowledge cannot
be realised. Therefore one who desires
knowledge and seeks liberation should
meditate on Brahman for a long time. (101)

यमो हि नियमस्त्यागो मौनं देशश्च कालता ।
आसनं मूलबन्धश्च देहसाम्यं च द्रक्स्थितिः ॥१०२॥

The control of the senses (*yama*), the
control of the intellect (*niyama*), the
avoidance of unreality (*tyaga*), spiritual
silence (*mauna*), place (*desa*), time (*kala*),
posture (*asana*), the subdual of the root-
cause (*mulabandha*), the equipoise of the
body (*deha-samya*), firmness of vision
(*drik-sthiti*).   (102)

प्राणसंयमनं वैव प्रत्याहारश्च धारणा ।

आत्मध्यानं समाधिश्च प्रोक्तान्यङ्गानि वै क्रमात् ॥

The control of life-forces (*pranayama*),
the withdrawal of consciousness (*pratyahara*), the holding of consciousness
(*dharana*), self-contemplation (*dhyana*),
and absorption (*samadhi*),—these in order,
are said to be the steps. (103)

सर्वं ब्रह्मेति विज्ञानादिन्द्रियग्रामसंयमः ।

यमोऽयमिति संप्रोक्तोऽभ्यसनीयो मुहुर्मुहुः ॥१०४॥

The control of all the senses by means
of the knowledge " all is Brahman " is
called *yama* and should be practised
again and again. (104)

सजातीयप्रवाहश्च विजातीयतिरस्कृतिः ।

नियमो हि परानन्दो नियमात्क्रियते बुधैः ॥१०५॥

The incessant flow of thought towards
all that relates to the self and the sub-
mergence of all that relates to the not-
self is called *niyama*. It imparts supreme
bliss and is assiduously practised by the
wise. (105)

त्यागः प्रपञ्चरूपस्य चिदात्मत्वावलोकनात् ।
त्यागो हि महतां पूज्यः सद्यो मोक्षमयो यतः ॥

Tyaga is the elimination of the pheno-
menon of the universe by realising the
self that is Brahman. *Tyaga* is venerated
even by the great, because it is of the
nature of instant liberation. (106)

यस्माद्वाचो निवर्तन्ते अप्राप्य मनसा सह ।
यन्मौनं योगिभिर्गम्यं तद्ब्रह्मेत्सर्वदा बुधः ॥ १०७ ॥

The wise man should always see himself as that *mauna* * from which word and
thought, not reaching it, turn away, but
which is attainable by *yogis*. (107)

वाचो यस्मान्निवर्तन्ते तद्वक्तुं केन शक्यते ।
प्रपञ्चो यदि वक्तव्यः सोऽपि शब्दविवर्जितः ॥

Who can speak of that from which all
words turn away? If the universe is to
be spoken of, even that is devoid of
words. † (108)

---

* Used here in the sense of *Brahman*.
† Since it is neither real nor non existent, hence
anirvachaniya.

इति वा तद्द्वेन्मौनं सतां सहजसंज्ञितम् ।
गिरा मौनं तु बालानां प्रयुक्तं ब्रह्मवादिभिः ॥१०९॥

The above may also be termed _mauna_
and is known as _sahaja_ among the
enlightened. The _mauna_ relating to
speech * has been ordained by the
teachers of Brahman for the ignorant.
(109)

आदावन्ते च मध्ये च जनो यस्मिन्न विद्यते ।
येनेदं सततं व्याप्तं स देशो विजनः स्मृतः ॥११०॥

That in which no individual existence
is possible at the beginning or end or in
the middle, that by which this universe
is at all times pervaded,—that is known
as the solitary place (_desa_). (110)

कलनात्सर्वभूतानां ब्रह्मादीनां निमेषतः ।
कालशब्देन निर्दिष्टो ह्यखण्डानन्द अद्वयः ॥१११॥

The secondless (_Brahman_) that is
infinite bliss is known as _kala_, because
by it are manifested, in the twinkling of
an eye, all creatures from the creator
downwards. (111)

---

* Literal silence.

सुखेनैव भवेद्यस्मिन्नजस्रं ब्रह्मचिन्तनम् ।
आसनं तद्विजानीयान्नेतरत्सुखनाशनम् ॥ ११२ ॥

That [conditional] in which Brahman
is incessantly contemplated with unmixed
bliss is known as *asana*, and not others*
which destroy bliss.   (112)

सिद्धं यत्सर्वभूतादि विश्वाधिष्ठानमव्ययम् ।
यस्मिन् सिद्धाः समाविष्टास्तद्वै सिद्धासनं विदुः ॥

The *siddha-asana** is the Immutable
which is the beginning of all beings and
the reality behind the universe, that in
which the perfected ever repose.   (113)

यन्मूलं सर्वभूतानां यन्मूलं चित्तबन्धनम् ।
मूलबन्धः सदा सेव्यो योग्योऽसौ राजयोगिनाम् ॥

That which is the root of all existence
and which has the control of the mind
for its root is the *mula-bandha*† which
should be adopted at all times, being fit
for the greatest of *yogis*.   (114)

---

* Postures and other conditions.
† The name of a particular posture in *yoga*.

अज्ञानां समतां विद्यात्समे ब्रह्मणि लीनताम् ।
नो चेन्नैव समानत्वमृजुत्वं शुष्कवृक्षवत् ॥ ११५ ॥

Absorption in the all-prevading Brahman is known as the equipoise of the limbs. Without such (absorption) there is no equipoise. Mere stiffness of body is like that of a withered tree. (115)

दृष्टिं ज्ञानमयीं कृत्वा पश्येद्ब्रह्ममयं जगत् ।
सा दृष्टिः परमोदारा न नासाग्रावलोकिनी ॥११६॥

Converting one's vision into one of knowledge, one should realise the whole world to be Brahman itself. This is the most advantageous vision (*drishti*) and not that which is directed to the tip of the nose. (116)

द्रष्टृदर्शनदृश्यानां विरामो यत्र वा भवेत् ।
दृष्टिस्तत्रैव कर्तव्या न नासाग्रावलोकिनी ॥ ११७ ॥

Or, the vision should be solely directed to that wherein ceases the distinction of seer, sight and object. It need not be directed to the tip of the nose. (117)

चित्तादिसर्वभावेषु ब्रह्मत्वेनैव भावनात् ।
निरोधः सर्ववृत्तीनां प्राणायामः स उच्यते ॥११८॥

Pranayama is the control of all life-
forces by realising naught but Brahman
in all things such as the mind etc.   (118)

निषेधनं प्रपञ्चस्य रेचकाख्यः समीरणः ।
ब्रह्मैवास्मीति या वृत्तिः पूरको वायुरीरितः ॥११९॥

The negation of the universe is the outgoing breath.   The thought "I am Brahman itself" is called the incoming breath.
(119)

ततस्तद्वृत्तिनैश्चल्यं कुम्भकः प्राणसंयमः ।
अयं चापि प्रबुद्धानामज्ञानां घ्राणपीडनम् ॥१२०॥

The permanence of that thought thereafter is the restrained breath. This is
the *pranayama* for the wise, while the
pressing of the nose is only for the
unknowing.   (120)

विषयेष्वात्मतां दृष्ट्वा मनसश्चिति मज्जनम् ।
प्रत्याहारः स विज्ञेयोऽभ्यसनीयो मुमुक्षुभिः ॥१२१॥

The merging of consciousness in Brahman by realising the self in all objects is
known as *pratyahara* and should be practised by all seekers after liberation. (121)

यत्र यत्र मनो याति ब्रह्मणस्तत्र दर्शनात् ।
मनसो धारणं चैव धारणा सा परा मता ॥१२२॥

Dharana, in its highest sense, is the holding of consciousness by realising Brahman wheresoever the consciousness reaches. (122)

ब्रह्मैवास्मीति सद्वृत्त्या निरालम्बतया स्थितिः ।
ध्यानशब्देन विख्याता परमानन्ददायिनी ॥१२३॥

The condition, wherein there is only the uncontradictable thought "I am Brahman itself" and there is no external hold, is denoted by the term *dhyana* and is productive of the highest bliss. (123)

निर्विकारतया वृत्त्या ब्रह्माकारतया पुनः ।
वृत्तिविस्तरणं सम्यक् समाधिर्ज्ञानसंज्ञकः ॥१२४॥

Samadhi, whose other name is knowledge, is the forgetfulness of all mental activity by first making thought changeless and then identifying the consciousness with Brahman. (124)

इमं चाकृत्रिमानन्दं तावत्साधु समभ्यसेत् ।
वश्यो यावत्क्षणात्पुंसः प्रयुक्तः सम्भवेत्स्वयम् ॥

One should earnestly practise this unconventional bliss until it will obediently

spring up of its own accord in an instant
at the will of the individual.   (125)

ततः साधननिर्मुक्तः सिद्धो भवति योगिराट् ।
तत्स्वरूपं न चैतस्य विषयो मनसो गिराम् ॥१२६॥

Then does one, independent of all
means, become a perfected being and the
greatest of *yogis*. But its real nature cannot be reached by one's word or thought.
                                        (126)

समाधौ क्रियमाणे तु विघ्ना आयान्ति वै बलात् ।
अनुसन्धानराहित्यमालस्यं भोगलालसम् ॥ १२७ ॥

While *samadhi* is being practised,
many impediments will perforce assail
one ; break of continuity, idleness, desire
for wordly pleasure.   (127)

लयस्तमश्च विक्षेपो रसास्वादश्च शून्यता ।
एवं यद्विघ्नबाहुल्यं त्याज्यं ब्रह्मविदा शनैः ॥१२८॥

Sleep, confusion, temptation, infatua-
tion, and a sense of blankness. These

and many other obstacles should be got
over, step by step, by the seeker after
Brahman. (128)

भाववृत्त्या हि भावत्वं शून्यवृत्त्या हि शून्यता ।
पूर्णवृत्त्या हि पूर्णत्वं तथा पूर्णत्वमभ्यसेत् ॥१२९॥

By the thought of an object, the consciousness becomes objective; by the
thought of blankness, the conciousness
becomes blank; and by the thought of
fullness (Brahman) it becomes full (Brahman). One should therefore practise ful-
ness. (129)

ये हि वृत्तिं जहत्येनां ब्रह्माख्यां पावनीं पराम् ।
वृथैव ते तु जीवन्ति पशुभिश्च समा नराः ॥१३०॥

Those that give up this highest and
purest Brahmic consciousness live in vain
and, though human, are like unto beasts.
(130)

ये हि वृत्तिं विजानन्ति ये ज्ञात्वा वर्धयन्त्यपि ।
ते वै सत्पुरुषा धन्या वन्द्यास्ते भुवनत्रये ॥१३१॥

They that have realised this consciousness and, having realised it, develop it
more and more, are the best of men,
fortunate, and venerable in all the three
worlds, (131)

येषां वृत्तिस्समा वृद्धा परिपक्का च सा पुनः ।
ते वै सद्ब्रह्मतां प्राप्ता नेतरे शब्दवादिनः ॥ १३२ ॥

They, in whom this consciousness
grows and also fructifies, attain identity
with the eternal Brahman, and not those
others who merely fight about words. (132)

कुशला ब्रह्मवार्तायां वृत्तिहीनास्सुरागिणः ।
ते ह्यज्ञानितमा नूनं पुनरायान्ति यान्ति च ॥१३३॥

These that are clever in their talk of
Brahman, but are devoid of this conciousness and are swayed by strong passions, are, indeed, the most ignorant
among men, and they again and again
pass through births and deaths.   (133)

निमेषार्धं न तिष्ठन्ति वृत्तिं ब्रह्ममयीं विना ।
यथा तिष्ठन्ति ब्रह्माद्याः सनकाद्याः शुकादयः ॥

The former (on the other hand) do not
remain for even half a second without the
Brahmic consciousness, in the same way as
Brahman* and others, Sanaka and others
Suka and others.   (134)

---

*The four-faced Creator.

कार्ये कारणताऽऽयाता कारणे न हि कार्यता ।
कारणत्वं ततो गच्छेत्कार्याभावे विचारतः ॥१३५॥

The nature of the cause passes into the
effect, but not the nature of the effect
into the cause. One should, therefore,
by diligent investigation, attain the
nature of the cause by eliminating the
effect.   (135)

अथ शुद्धं भवेद्वस्तु यद्वै वाचामगोचरम् ।
द्रष्टव्यं मृद्घटेनैव दृष्टान्तेन पुनः पुनः ॥ १३६ ॥

Then will shine the absolutely real
(self) that is beyond the scope of words.
This should be understood again and
again by the illustration of the earthen
vessel.*   (136)

अनेनैव प्रकारेण वृत्तिर्ब्रह्मात्मिका भवेत् ।
उदेति शुद्धचित्तानां वृत्तिज्ञानं ततः परम् ॥ १३७ ॥

In this manner do the understanding
(*vritti*) of Brahman and, thereafter, the
Brahmic consciousness (*v r i t t i-j n a n a*)
spring up in the pure-minded.   (137)

---

*The earthen vessel and the clay are illustrations
of effect and cause respectively. One can only see
the clay in the vessel, by eliminating the name and
form of the vessel.

कारणं व्यतिरेकेण पुमानादौ विलोकयेत् ।
अन्वयेन पुनस्तद्धि कार्ये नित्यं प्रपश्यति ॥ १३८ ॥

One should first see the cause as distinct from the effect, and should then, at
all times, realise the cause as inherent in
the effect itself.   (138)

कार्ये हि कारणं पश्येत्पश्चात्कार्यं विसर्जयेत् ।
कारणत्वं ततो गच्छेदवशिष्टं भवेन्मुनिः ॥ १३९ ॥

One should see the cause in the effect,
and should then eliminate the effect. The
cause, as such, will vanish (of its own
accord). What then remains, that the
sage becomes.   (139)

भावितं तीव्रवेगेन वस्तु यन्निश्चयात्मना ।
पुमांस्तद्धि भवेच्छीघ्रं ज्ञेयं भ्रमरकीटवत् ॥ १४० ॥

For, one soon becomes that which he
contemplates with extreme assiduity and
absolute certainty This should be understood by the illustration of the wasp
and the worm.*   (140)

---

*It is the popular belief that the worm in the wasp s
nest develops into a wasp by its constant expectation
of the wasp's return.

अदृश्यं भावरूपं 'च सर्वमेतच्चिदात्मकम् ।
सावधानतया नित्यं खात्मानं भावयेद्बुधः ॥ १४१ ॥

The wise man, at all times, should
attentively meditate upon his own self
which, though unseen, is yet the only
reality, and, though manifest as the external universe, is yet of the nature of
subjective consciousness.   (141)

दृश्यं ह्यदृश्यतां नीत्वा ब्रह्माकरेण चिन्तयेत् ।
विद्वान्नित्यसुखे तिष्ठेद्धिया चिद्रसपूर्णया ॥ १४२ ॥

Having turned the visible into the invisible, one should realise everything to
be Brahman itself. The wise man should
then dwell in eternal bliss with his mind
full of the essence of pure consciousness.
                                     (142)

एभिरङ्गैः समायुक्तो राजयोग उदाहृतः ।
किञ्चित्पक्वकषायाणां हठयोगेन संयुतः ॥ १४३ ॥

This is known as the *raja-yoga*, consisting of the steps mentioned above. With
this should be combined the *hatha-yoga*,
for those whose passions have only been
partially eradicated.   (143)

परिपक्वं मनो येषां केवलोऽयं न सिद्धिदः ।
गुरुदैवतभक्तानां सर्वेषां सुलभो जवात् ॥ १४४ ॥

To those, however, whose minds are
fully ripe, the above *yoga* is by itself
productive of perfection. It is easily and
speedily attainable by all who have faith
in the teacher and in the Lord.   (144)

॥ इत्यपरोक्षानुभूतिः समाप्ता ॥

Thus ends DIRECT REALISATION.

॥ शतश्लोकी ॥

THE CENTURY OF VERSES

दृष्टान्तो नैव दृष्टस्त्रिभुवनजठरे सद्गुरोर्ज्ञानदातुः
स्पर्शश्चेत्तत्र कल्प्यः स नयति यदहो स्वर्णतामश्ममसारम् ।
न स्पर्शत्वं तथाऽपि श्रितचरणयुगे सद्गुरुः स्वीयशिष्ये
स्वीयं साम्यं विधत्ते भवति निरुपमस्तेन वाऽलौकि-
[कोऽपि ॥ १ ॥

There is no known comparison in all
the three worlds for the venerable teacher
that bestows knowledge. If the philosopher's stone be assumed as such, it only
turns iron into gold, but alas! cannot con-
vert it into philosopher's stone. The
venerable teacher, on the other hand,
creates equality with himself in the disciple that takes refuge in his feet. He
is therefore peerless, nay, even transcendental. (1)

यद्वच्छीखण्डवृक्षप्रसृतपरिमलेनाभितोऽन्येऽपि वृक्षाः
शश्वत्सौगन्ध्यभाजोऽप्यतनुतनुभृतां तापमुन्मूलयन्ति ।
आचार्यात्लब्धबोधा अपि विधिवशतः सन्निधौ संस्थि-
[तानां
त्रेधा तापं च पापं सकरुणहृदयाः स्वोक्तिभिः क्षाल-
[यन्ति ॥ २ ॥

Just as, by virtue of the fragrance dif-
fused by a sandal tree, other trees around
it are also full of fragrance at all times
and afford shelter from heat to diverse
beings, so do they that have derived
wisdom from the teacher, with hearts
full of mercy, emancipate, by their
teachings, all those who are fortunate
enough to stand in their presence, from
the three kinds of misery * and the three
kinds of sin. †   (2)

आत्मानात्मप्रतीतिः प्रथममभिहिता सत्यमिथ्यात्वयो-

[गात्

द्वेधा ब्रह्मप्रतीतिर्निगमनिगदिता स्वानुभूत्योपपत्त्या ।

आद्या देहानुबन्धाद्भवति तदपरा सा च सर्वात्मकत्वात्

आदौ ब्रह्माहमस्मीत्यनुभव उदिते खल्विदं ब्रह्म पश्चात्॥

At the outset is enunciated the perception of the self and of the not-self by
means, respectively, of true knowledge
and illusion. Thus does scripture speak
of the knowledge of Brahman as two-

---

*Adhyatmika or bodily ailments, adhibhautika or
danger from other beings such as wild animals. and
adhidaivika or danger from forces of nature such as
earthquakes, floods, etc.

† Sins of body, speech and mind.

fold, namely, by means of experience relating to oneself (*savannbhuti*) and by conclusive certainty (*upapatti*). The former arises in correlation to bodily limitation, while the latter arises out of universality ; at first springs up the experience "I am Brahman", and then "*All this* is Brahman."   (3)

आत्मा चिद्वित्सुखात्माऽनुभवपरिचितः सर्वेदेहादि-
[यन्ता
सत्येवं मूढबुद्धिर्भजति ननु जनोऽनित्यदेहात्मबुद्धिम् ।
बाह्योऽस्थिस्नायुमज्जापलरुधिरवसाचर्ममेदोयुगन्तः
विण्मूत्रश्लेष्मपूर्णं स्वपरवपुरहो संविदित्वाऽपि भूयः ॥

The nature of the self is <u>consciousness,</u> <u>knowledge</u> ,and <u>bliss.</u> It can be known by direct realisation. It is the inspiring soul in all bodies, (senses), etc. And yet, the utterly ignorant person mistakes the transient body for the soul, although he knows again and again that the body, whether his own or another's is externally composed of bones, tendon, marrow, flesh, blood, nerves, skin and fat, and internally full of ordure, urine and phlegm.   (4)

देहस्त्रीपुत्रमित्रानुचरहयवृषास्तोषहेतुर्ममेतथं
सर्वे स्वायुर्नेयन्ति प्रथितमलममी मांसमीमांसयेह ।
एते जीवन्ति येन व्यवहृतिपटवो येन सौभाग्यभाजः
तं प्राणाधीशमन्तर्गतममृतममुं नैब मीमांसयन्ति ॥५॥

All these beings spend the whole of
their valuable life-time on earth as followers of the philosophy of the flesh,
imagining: "The body, wife, sons,
friends. servants, horses, cattle,—these
are the sources of my happiness." They
fail to understand that inner, immortal
Lord of Life, by whom they live, by
whom they are rendered fit for the duties
of life and by whom they are endowed
with prosperity.   (5)

कश्चित्कीटः कथञ्चित्पटुमतिरभितः कण्टकानां कुटीरं
कुर्वंस्तेनैव साकं व्यवहृतिविधये चेष्टते यावदायुः ।
तद्वज्जीवोऽपि नानाचरितसमुदितैः कर्मभिः स्थूलदेहं
निर्मायात्रैव तिष्ठन्नुदिनममुना साकमभ्येति भूमौ ॥६॥

Just as a sagacious insect (e.g., the silk-
worm) builds, by its own efforts, a cocoon
around itself and, jointly therewith,
moves about throughout its life in the

discharge of its activities, so does the
individual soul, by means of the fruits of
various actions, build up a physical body
and, remaining therein, move about along
with it, day by day, on earth.   (6)

स्वीकुर्वन्व्याघ्रवेषं खजठरभृतये भीषयन्यश्च मुग्धान्
मत्वा व्याघ्रोऽहमित्थं स नरपशुमुखान्बाधते किं नु
[सत्त्वान्

मत्वा स्त्रीवेषधारी स्त्र्यहमिति कुरुते किं नटो भर्तुरिच्छां
तद्वच्छारीर आत्मा पृथगनुभवतो देहतो यः स साक्षी॥

Does a person, who assumes the mask
of a tiger for his livelihood and frightens
the young ones, injure any man, beast or
other living being, under the impression
that he is a tiger? Or, does the actor,
playing a woman's part, pant for a hus-
band, imagining himself to be a woman?
So is the self conditioned by the body,
but, being different from the body and
from experience, is only the witness.   (7)

स्वं बालं रोदमानं चिरतरसमयं शान्तिमानेतुमग्रे
द्राक्षं खार्जूरमाम्रं सुकदलमथवा योजयत्यम्बिकाऽस्य ।
तद्वच्चेतोऽतिमूढं बहुजननभवान्मौल्यसंस्कारयोगात्
बोधोपायैरनेकैरवशमुपनिषद्बोधयामास सम्यक् ॥८॥

Just as a mother, in order to pacify her
child that has been weeping for a very
long time, places before it a grape, a date,
a mango, or a good plantain fruit, so,
well has the *upanishad*, by various teaching expedients, enlightened the utterly
ignorant mind that wanders restlessly in
consequence of the faculty of delusion
acquired in numerous lives.   (8)

यत्प्रीया प्रीतिमात्रं तनुयुवतितनूजार्थमुख्यं स तस्मात्
प्रेयानात्माऽथ शोकास्पदमितरदतः प्रेय एतत्कथं स्यात् ।
भार्यादं जीवितार्थे वितरति च वपुः स्वात्मनः श्रेय
                                        [इच्छन्
तस्मादात्मानमेव   प्रियमधिकमुपासीत   विद्वान्न
                                        [चान्यत् ॥ ९ ॥

That self, by reason of which being
dear, all things like the body, wife, children and wealth, are dear, must itself be
dearer than those things. Those things,
on the other hand, are sources of misery.
How, then, can they be dearer (than the
self)? For the sake of saving one's own
life, one gives up even his wife and
others, and, for the good of one's own
self, one gives up even one's own body.
The wise should therefore cherish the

self as the most beloved and not anything
else.   (9)

यस्माद्यावत्प्रियं स्यादिह हि विषयतस्तावदस्मिन्प्रियत्वं
यावद्दुःखं च यस्माद्भवति खलु ततस्तावदेवाप्रियत्वम् ।
नैकस्मिन्सर्वकालेऽस्त्युभयमपि कदाप्यप्रियोऽपिप्रियः
                                                   [स्यात्
प्रेयानप्यप्रियो वा सततमपि ततः प्रेयआत्माख्यवस्तु ॥

As long as one derives pleasure from
an object, so long is it beloved; and as
long as it gives rise to pain, so long is it
disliked. Neither pleasantness nor un-
pleasantness resides at all times in the
same object. Sometimes what is unpleasant might become pleasant, and what is
very pleasant might become unpleasant.
The reality known as the self is, therefore, the most beloved at all times.   (10)

श्रेयश्च प्रेयश्च लोके द्विविधमभिहितं काम्यमात्यन्तिकं च
काम्यं दुःखैकबीजं क्षणलवविरसं तच्चिकीर्षन्ति मन्दाः ।
ब्रह्मैवात्यन्तिकं यन्निरतिशयसुखस्यास्पदं संश्रयन्ते
तत्त्वज्ञास्तच्च काठोपनिषदभिहितं षड्विधायां च
                                                   [वल्ल्याम् ॥ ११ ॥

What is preferable in the world and
what is pleasant are each said to be of

two kinds, namely, that which is actuated by desire and that which is absolute.
That which is actuated by desire is the
sole source of sorrow and becomes insipid
in an instant; it is sought after by the
ignorant. Brahman alone is the absolute,
being the repository of unsurpassed bliss;
therein do they that know the truth take
refuge. This is declared in the six divisions (*valli*) of the Kathopanishad. (11)

आत्माम्भोधेस्तरङ्गोऽस्म्यहमिति गमने भावयन्नासनस्थः
संवित्सूत्रानुविद्धो मणिरहमिति वाऽस्मीन्द्रियार्थप्रतीतौ।
द्रष्टोऽस्म्यात्मावलोकादिति शयनविधौ मग्न आनन्द-
[सिन्धौ
अन्तर्निष्ठे मुमुक्षुः स खलु तनुभृतां यो नयत्येवमायुः ॥

Feeling, while going about, that he is a
wave of the ocean of the self: while sitting, that he is a bead strung on the
thread of universal consciousness: while
perceiving objects of sense, that he is
realising himself by perceiving the self:
and, while sleeping, that he is drowned
in the ocean of bliss;—he who, inwardly
constant, spends his whole life thus is,
among all men, the real seeker of liberation.
(12)

वैराजव्यष्टिरूपं जगदखिलमिदं नामरूपात्मकं स्यात्
अन्तःस्थप्राणमुख्यात्प्रचलति च पुनर्वेत्ति सर्वान्पदा-
[र्थान् ।
नायं कर्ता न भोक्ता सवितृवदिति यो ज्ञानविज्ञानपूर्णः
साक्षादित्थं विजानन्व्यवहरति परात्मानुसन्धान-
[पूर्वम् ॥ १३ ॥

All this world, consisting of name and
form, is only the particular manifestation
(*vyashti*) of the universal Substance
(*viraj*) ; it moves and knows all objects
by virtue of the primal life (*mukhya-
prana*), that inspires it. This self, like
the sun, is neither the doer nor the
enjoyer.—Thus, directly realising, does
he that is full of knowledge and realisation live his life, through incessant contemplation of the supreme self. (13)

नैवेवं ज्ञानगर्भं द्विविधमभिहितं तत्र वैराग्यमाद्यं
प्रायो दुःखावलोकाद्भवति गृहसुहृत्पुत्रवित्तेषणादेः ।
अन्यज्ज्ञानोपदेशाद्युदितविषये वान्तवद्धेयता स्यात्
प्रत्रज्याऽपि द्विधा स्यान्नियमितमनसां देहतो गेहतश्च ॥

Non-attachment (*vairagya*) is declared
to be of two kinds, namely, that which

springs from disgust (*nirveda*) and that
which is inspired by knowledge. The
former arises from the observation that
desires, such as for home or friends or
sons or wealth, generally end in sorrow;
while the latter is the rejection of the
above-mentioned things, by virtue of the
wisdom imparted, as if they were vomit-
ted matter. Renunciation too is of two
kinds for those of subdued mind, namely,
that of the body and that of the home.

(14)

यः कश्चित्सौख्यहेतोरिजगति यतते नैव दुःखस्य हेतोः
देहेऽहन्ता तदुत्था खविषयममता चेति दुःखास्पदे द्वे ।
ज्ञान्नोगाभिघाताद्यनुभवति यतोऽनित्यदेहात्मबुद्धिः
भार्यापुत्रार्थनाशे विपदमथ परामेति नारातिनाशे १५

Every one in all the three worlds strives
for happiness, and not at all for misery.
The two sources of misery are the sense
of I-ness in the body and the sense of
mineness, arising therefrom, in the objects of one's own consciousness; for,
even the learned man undergoes suffering
from disease or assault by mistaking the
transient body for the self, and experi-

ences extreme sorrow at the loss of wife, son or wealth, but not at the loss of an enemy.*　　(15)

तिष्ठन्गेहे गृहेशोऽप्यतिथिरिव निजं धाम गन्तुं चिकीर्षुः
देहस्थं दुःखसौख्यं न भजति सहसा निर्ममत्वाभिमानः।
आयात्रायास्यतीदं जलदपटलवच्चात् यास्यत्यवश्यं
देहाद्यं सर्वमेव प्रविदितविशयो यश्च तिष्ठत्ययत्नः १६

Although dwelling in the houses as the head of the family, he who is devoid of the feeling of mine-ness remains therein like a guest longing to reach his destination,† and feels not, with fervour, the happiness or the misery residing in the body. What must happen, whether it be the body or anything else, will surely happen, and what must be lost, will surely be lost, like the gathering of clouds. He who knows this truth remains at ease.　　(16)

शक्त्या निर्मोकतः स्वादुद्रहिरिव यः प्रत्रजन्स्वीयगेहात्
छायां मार्गेद्रुमोत्थां पथिक इव मनाक् संश्रयेद्देहसं-
[स्थाम्।
क्षुत्पर्याप्तं तरुभ्यः पतितफलमयं प्रार्थयेद्वैद्यमन्नं
स्वात्मारामं प्रवेष्टं स खलु सुखमयं प्रत्रजेद्देहतोऽपि॥

---

* Because there is no I-ness or mine-ness in the case of an enemy.

† The Brahman.

He who, by strength of will, escapes from his own home like a snake out of its slough, might occasionally attend to the sustenance of his body like a traveller resorting to the shade of a wayside tree, but should only beg of trees so much food, in the shape of fruits fallen of their own accord, as would be enough to appease his hunger. He should also go forth from his body in order to enter the garden of his own self that is full of bliss.   (17)

कामो बुद्धावुदेति प्रथममिह मनस्युद्दिशत्यर्थजातं
तद्ब्रह्मातीन्द्रियास्यैस्तदनधिगमतः क्रोध आविर्भवेच्च ।
प्राप्तावर्थस्य संरक्षणमतिरुदितो लोभ एतत्त्रयं स्यात्
सर्वेषां पातहेतुस्तदिह मतिमता त्याज्यमध्यात्मयोगात् ॥

There first arises, in the mind, desire. It then directs the mind to various objects. The mind then grasps those objects through the medium of the senses. When an object is not attained, there springs up anger. When an object is attained, there arises greed in the shape of eagerness to preserve that object. These three are the cause of every one's ruin. The wise should therefore

shun them by constant meditation upon
the self.   (18)

दानं ब्रह्मार्पणं यत्क्रियत इह नृभिः स्वात्क्षमाऽक्रोधसंज्ञा
श्रद्धाऽऽस्तिक्यं च सत्यं सदिति परमतः सेतुसंज्ञं
[चतुष्कम् ।
तत्स्याद्बन्धाय जन्तोरिति चतुर इमान्दानपूर्वैश्चतुर्भिः
तीर्त्वा श्रेयोऽमृतं च श्रयत इह नरः स्वर्गतिं ज्योतिरा-
[त्मिम् ॥ १९ ॥

That is a gift which is made by men as
a dedication to Brahman ; patience is the
absence of anger ; faith ·is the belief in
the existence of the self ; and the reality
is Brahman (*sat*). The four opposites of
these are known as the barriers (*setu*), and
tend to the bondage of every being. One
should therefore overcome these barriers
by means of the four gifts, etc., aforesaid,
and should thereby attain happiness,
immortality, heavenward progress, and
the realisation of the light.   (19)

अन्नं देवातिथिभ्योऽर्पितममृतमिदं चान्यथा मोघमन्नं
यच्चात्मार्थं विधत्ते तदिह निगदितं मृत्युरूपं हि तस्य ।
लोकेऽसौ केवलाघो भवति तनुभृता केवलादी च यः
[स्यात्
त्यक्त्वा प्राणाग्निहोत्रं विधिवदनुदिनं योऽश्नुते सोऽपि
[मर्त्यः ॥ २० ॥

Food that is dedicated to the Lord and
to guests tends to immortality; otherwise,
the food is useless. So, too, food that is
cooked for one's own sake is said to be
one's death. He, too, among men, who
eats by himself, becomes wholly sinful in
this world. And he, too, who eats daily
without the prescribed consecration of
the food to the fire of life, remains a
mortal.   (20)

लोको भोजस्स एवार्पयति गृहगतायार्थिनेऽन्नं कृशाय
यस्तस्मै पूर्णमन्नं भवति मखविधौ जायतेऽजातशत्रुः ।
सख्ये नान्नार्थिने योऽर्पयति न स सखा सेवमानाय
[नित्यं
संसक्तायान्नमस्माद्विमुख इव परावृत्तिमिच्छेत्कदर्यात् ॥

He alone, in the world, is the giver who
offers food to the famished mendicant
that comes to his house. To such an one
there is plenty of food for sacrifice, and
he becomes one that has no enemy. He,
on the other hand, who does not offer
food even to the friend that has constantly served him with attachment for
the sake of food, is not a friend. From
such a miser one should be anxious to

turn away, as it were, out of disregard.

(21)

स्वाज्ञानज्ञानहेतू जगदुदयलयौ सर्वसाधारणौ स्तः
जीवेश्वास्खर्णगर्भं श्रुतय इति जगुर्हूयते स्वप्रबोधे ।
विश्वं ब्रह्मण्यबोधे जगति पुनरिदं हूयते ब्रह्म यद्वत्
शुक्तौ रौप्यं च रौप्येऽधिकरणमथवा हूयतेऽन्योन्यमो-
[हात् ॥ २२ ॥

The manifestation and the dissolution of the universe have, for their respective cause, the ignorance or the knowledge of the self, and are applicable to all beings from the creator (*hiranya-garbha*) downwards,—so do the Vedas declare. When the self is realised, the universe is sacrificed* into Brahman, and, when the self is not realised, this Brahman is again sacrificed into the universe, in the same way as the (illusory) silver disappears into the mother-of-pearl and the real

---

*These two sacrifices stand respectively for the dissolution of the manifest or apparent into the unmanifest or real, and the opposite process of the unmanifest seemingly becoming the manifest.

substance (the mother-of-pearl into the illusory) silver owing to the non-recognition of each of them in turn.   (22)

तुच्छत्वाज्ञासदासीद्रगनकुसुमवद्भेदकं नो सदासीत्
किन्त्वाभ्यामन्यदासीद्व्यवहतिगतिसज्ञास लोकस्तदा-
                                        [नीम्
किन्त्ववर्गेव शुक्तौ रजतवदपरो नो विराड् व्योमपूर्वः
शर्मण्यात्मन्यथैतत्कुहकसलिलवत्कि भवेदावरीवः २३

Then was not non-entity, that being absolutely non-existent like the sky-flower; nor was then any entity that could divide. But something then was, different from these two. Then was not the universe as it (now) exists in its phenomenal condition; and yet it already existed differently, as the (illusory) silver already exists in the mother-of-pearl. Nor was then the primordial (cosmic) substance (*virat*) sprung from other. For, what is there, like unto the water produced by magic, that can veil the unconditioned self?   (23)

---

*This verse deals with the cause of the universe, *i.e.*, what was before creation.

बन्धो जन्मात्ययात्मा यदि न पुनरभूर्त्तर्हि मोक्षोऽपि

[नासीत्

यद्द्रात्रिर्दिनं वा न भवति तरणौ किन्तु दृग्दोष एषः ।

अप्राणं शुद्धमेकं समभवदथ तन्मायया कर्तृसंज्ञं

तस्मादन्यच्च नासीत्परिवृतमजया जीवभूतं तदेव ॥२४॥

If there was no bondage in the shape
of origin and dissolution, neither was
there liberation ; just as there is neither
night nor day in the sun, for, it is only a
limitation of vision. The One, motionless and unconditioned, then became, by
its own power of illusion (*maya*), that
which is known as the maker (*Kartri*)*.
And there was naught else than that.
That alone, veiled by the unborn, became
the individual soul.   (24)

प्रागासीद्द्वावरूपं तम इति तमसा गूढमस्मादतर्क्यं

क्षीरान्तर्यद्वदम्भो जनिरिह जगतो नामरूपात्मकस्य ।

कामाद्धातुः सिसृक्षोरनुगतजगतः कर्मभिः सम्प्रवृत्तात्

रेतोरूपैर्मनोभिः प्रथममनुगतैः सन्ततैः कार्यमाणै: २५

In the beginning was darkness,* as an
entity. Thus veiled by darkness, naught
could then be seen, like the water that is

---

*otherwise known as *Hiranya-garbha*.   † Maya.

contained in milk. The birth of this universe, consisting of name and form, was
by virtue of the will of the Creator
desiring to create,—this will being
induced by the actions (*karmabhih*) of a
continuous (*anugata*) universe constantly
inspired by minds that are also continuous in a germinal form.   (25)

चत्वारोऽस्याः कपर्दा युवतिरथ भवेन्नूतना निलयमेषा
माया वा पेशला स्याद्घटितघटनापाटवं याति यस्मात् ।
स्यादारम्भे घृतास्या श्रुतिभववयुनान्येवमाच्छादयन्ती
तस्यामेतौ सुपर्णाविव परपुरुषौ तिष्ठतोऽर्थप्रतीया २६

This (goddess of) illusion (*maya*) has
four crests. * She is always fresh and
therefore ever young.   She is skilful,
because she is an expert in accomplishing even the impossible. She is sweet-
mouthed ‡ at the outset. Thus, too, she
veils the knowledge derivable from the
upanishads. In her dwell, like two birds,
the supreme self and the individual soul,
for they alone make all things manifest.
                                      (26)

---

* *Ajnana*, nescience.   † *i.e.* , eminent qualities.

† *Ghritasya*, lit. ghee-mouthed, *i.e.* tempting at first
but finally leading to ruin.

एकस्तत्रास्यसङ्गस्तदनु तदपरोऽज्ञानसिन्धुं प्रविष्टो
विस्मृत्यात्मस्वरूपं स विविधजगदाकारमाभासमैक्षत् ।
बुद्ध्याऽन्तर्यावदैक्षद्विसृजति तमसा सोऽपि तामेवमेकः
तावद्विप्रास्तमेकं कथमपि बहुधा कल्पयन्ति स्ववाग्भिः ॥

Of these two, the former remains unattached, while the latter, on the other
hand, falling into the ocean of ignorance
and forgetting the real nature of the self,
perceived the apparition of these various
worlds. But no sooner has he turned his
consciousness within himself than the
unborn (*maya*) abandons him and he
abandons her. There is, thus, One only.
But the wise, somehow, render that One
variously by their teachings.*   (27)

नायाति प्रत्यगात्मा प्रजननसमये नैव यात्यन्तकाले
यत्सोऽखण्डोऽस्ति लैङ्गं मन इह विशति प्रत्रजत्यूर्ध्व-
[सर्वाक्

तत्कार्यं स्थूलतां वा न भजति वपुषः किन्तु संस्कारजाते
तेजोमात्रा गृहीत्वा व्रजति पुनरिहायाति तैस्तैस्सहैव ॥

The inner self neither comes in at the
time of birth, nor goes away at the time

---

*For purposes of instruction, and not as repre-
senting the ultimate truth.

of death; for it is infinite. But it is the
mind with the subtle body that enters
thus and goes forth afterwards. The
mind does not reproduce in itself the
leanness or the stoutness of the gross
body. But it departs, taking with it the
two sets * of tendencies (*samskara*) and
the measures of light (*tejo-matrah*) †, and
returns again to this world along with
these very appendages. (28)

आसीत्पूर्वं सुबन्धुर्भृशमवनिसुरो यः पुरोधाः सनातेः

ब्राह्यात्कूटाभिचारात्स खलु मृतिमितस्तन्मनोऽगात्कृ-

[तान्तम् ।

तद्भ्राता श्रौतमन्त्रैः पुनरनयदिति प्राह सूक्तेन वेदः

तस्मादात्माभियुक्तं व्रजति ननु मनः कर्हिचिन्नान्त-

[रात्मा ॥ २९ ॥

There was, of old, a venereble Brah-
mana, named Subandhu, who was the
priest of (king) Sanati; he having died
by the deceitful incantations of some
Brahmanas, his mind went to (the abode
of the god of) death, and his brother
brought it back by means of Vedic
hymns,—so says the Veda. It follows
from this that the mind alone as rela-

---

*Good and evil.
† The five senses of perception and the life-forces
in their subtlest form.

ted to the self, goes forth and not the
inner self, in any case.   (29)

एको निष्कम्प आत्मा प्रचलति मनसा धावमानेन
[तस्मिन्

तिष्ठन्नमेऽथ पश्चान्न हि तमनुगतं जान्ते चक्षुरादाः ।

यद्वत्पाथस्तरङ्गैः प्रचलति परितो धावमानैस्तदन्तः

प्राक्पश्चादस्ति तेषां पवनसमुदितैस्तैः प्रशान्तैर्यथावत् ॥

The one motionless self moves with the
wandering mind, remain in it, and is also
both before and behind it   But although
it is thus present throughout, the eye and
other senses know it not, Water, for
instance, moves about with the rolling
waves raised by the wind, is in them and
before them by and behind them; and
when the waves are still, is, as it ever is.
                                             (30)

एकाक्यासीत्स पूर्वं मृगयति विषयानानुपूर्व्याऽन्तरात्मा
जाया मे स्यात्प्रजा वा धनमुपकरणं कर्म कुर्वस्तदर्थम् ।
क्लेशैः प्राणावशेषैर्मेहर्दपि मनुते नान्यदस्मादरीयः
त्वेकालाभेऽप्यकृत्स्नो मृत इव विरमत्येकहान्याऽ-
[कृतार्थः ॥ ३१ ॥

The inner self was, at first, by itself.
Then it seeks objects of enjoyment one
after another: "Let me have wife and
children and wealth to support them."

For their sake, the man works with very
many difficulties even at the risk of his
life, and not deem anything else to be
higher or greater than them. Even if
any one of them is not gained. he feels
himself to be incomplete and is as
inactive as if he were dead; so too, even
if any one of them is lost, he feels he has
entirely missed his purpose.   (31)

नासीत्पूर्वे न पश्चादतनुदिनकराच्छादको वारिवाहः

दृश्यःकिन्त्वन्तराऽसौ स्थगयति स दृशं पश्यतो नार्के-
[बिम्बम् ।

नो चेदेवं विनाऽर्कं जलधरपटलं भासते तर्हि कस्मात्
तद्विद्विश्रं विधत्ते दृशमथ न परं भासकं चालकं खम् ॥

The cloud that hides the huge sun has
not existed (ever) before, nor will exist
(ever) thereafter, but is visible only
during that interval. And it obstructs
the vision of the spectator and not the
solar orb : for, if it were not so, how can
the group of clouds be visible without the
sun ? In this manner does the universe
(visva) * veil the understanding and not
the supreme (self) that is its† own
illuminer and inspirer.   (32)

---

* Appearance or phenomenal existence.
† Of the universe.

भुञ्जानःस्वप्नराज्यं स सकलविभवो जागरं प्राप्य भूयः ।
राज्यभ्रष्टोऽहमित्थं न भजति विषमं तन्मृषा मन्यमानः ।
स्वप्ने कुर्वन्नगम्यागमनमुखमघं तेन न प्रत्यवायी
तद्वज्जाग्रद्दशायां व्यवहृतिमखिलां स्वप्नवद्विस्मरेच्चेत् ॥

Having, in dream, ruled a kingdom
with all the glories thereof, one does not
on waking thereafter, feel sorry that he
has lost his kingdom, knowing, as he
does, that it was unreal. Nor does one
become liable to punishment by commit-
ting adultery or other evil deed in dream.
So will it be, if one should forget all the
activities of his waking state like dreams.
(33)

स्वाप्नावस्थानुभूतं शुभमथ विषमं तन्मृषा जागरे स्यात्
जाग्रत्यां स्थूलदेहव्यवहृतिविषयं तन्मृषा स्वापकाले ।
इत्थं मिथ्यात्वसिद्धावनिशमुभयधा सज्जते तत्र मूढः
सत्ये तद्भासकेऽस्मिन्निह हि कुत इदं तन्न विद्मो वयं
[हि ॥ ३४ ॥

The pleasure or pain experienced in the
dream-state becomes unreal on waking,
and the objects towards which the activities of the physical body are directed
in the waking state become unreal during

sleep. But, although unreality is thus
established in both ways, the ignorant
person still clings to it* although its
illuminer is the self (satya). Surely, we
are not aware why this should be so. (34)

जीवन्तं जाग्रतीह स्वजनमथ मृतं स्वप्नकाले निरीक्ष्य

निर्वेदं यायकसान्मृतममृतमसुं वीक्ष्य हर्षं प्रयाति ।

स्मृत्वाऽप्येतस्य जन्तोर्निधनमसुयुतिं भाषते तेन साकं

सत्येवं भाति भूयोऽल्पकसमयवशात्सत्यता वा

[मृषात्वम् ॥ ३५ ॥

One is filled with sudden grief on
seeing the death, in one's dream, of a
relation that lives in one's waking state.
So, too, does one feel happy by seeing
alive, in dream, one that was dead in the
waking state. And although one re-
members (in dream) the death or the life
of the individual (in one's waking condition), he nevertheless converses with
him. This being so, reality or unreality
depends only on the length or shortness
of time.† (35)

---

*Bodily enjoyment.

† The seeming reality of waking experiences and
the unreality of dreams are distinguifhed only by the
difference of their duration. From the ultimate
standpoint, however, both are unreal.

स्वाप्रस्त्रीसङ्गसौख्यादपि भृशमसतो याच रेतश्च्युतिः
[स्यात्

सा दृश्या तद्वदेतत्स्फुरति जगदसत्कारणं सत्यकल्पम् ।
स्वप्ने सत्यः पुमान्स्याद्युवतिरिह मृषैवानयोः संयुतिश्च
प्रातः शुक्रेण वस्त्रोपहतिरिति यतः कल्पनामूलमेतत् ॥

Although the pleasure of meeting a
woman in dream is extremely unreal, yet
the discharge resulting therefrom is
visible. In the same way does the universe appear as almost real, although it
has sprung from unreality. The man in
the (above) dream may be real, but the
woman and her company are only unreal,
and yet the cloth is actually soiled in the
morning by the discharge. All this
universe, therefore, has imagination
(*kalpana*)* for its root-clause.   (36)

पश्यत्यारामममस्य प्रतिदिवसममी जन्तवः स्वापकाले
पश्यत्येनं न कश्चित्करणगणमृते मायया क्रीडमानम् ।
जाग्रत्यर्थव्रजानामथ च तनुभृतां भासकं चालकं वा
नो जानीते सुषुप्तौ परमसुखमयं कश्चिदाश्चर्यमेतत् ॥

All persons witness the sport of this
(self) every day in the dream-state, and

*Illusion, nescience. The self is compared to the
man, illusion to the woman and the manifest universe
to the discharge.

yet no one sees that (self) itself sporting
with illusion (*maya*) without any of the
organs of sense.* Nor does any one
realise it, in the waking state, as the
illuminer of all objects and the inspirer
of all creatures, nor, in deep sleep, as
that which is full of supreme bliss.   This
is wonderful !   (37)

स्वप्ने मन्त्रोपदेशः श्रवणपरिचितः सत्य एष प्रबोधे

स्वाप्रादेव प्रसादादभिलषितफलं सत्यतां प्रातरेति ।

सत्यप्राप्तिस्त्वसत्यादपि भवति तथा किञ्च तत्त्वप्रकाशं

येनेदं भाति सर्वं चरमचरमथोच्चावचं दृश्यजातम् ३८

The revelation of a sacred word (*mantra*)
heard in dream becomes real on waking :
and as the result of a benediction in
dream, the desired object is actually
attained in the morning. Thus the real
may spring up even from the unreal.†
Further, that (self) alone is self-resplendent by which are manifested all
animate and inanimate things, the entire

---

*Since, the experiences of the dream-state are
independent of the senses.

† Therefore although all phenomena are illusory,
the realisation of Brahman is not an illusion.

variety of perceivable objects, nay, the
whole universe itself.   (38)

मध्यप्राणं सुषुप्तौ स्वजनिमनुविशन्त्यग्निसूर्योदयोऽमी

वागाद्याः प्राणवायुं तदिह निगदिता ग्लानिरेषां न
[वायोः ।

तेभ्यो द्दश्यावभासो भ्रम इति विदितः शुक्तिकारौप्य-
[कल्पः

प्राणायामव्रतं तच्छ्रुतिशिरसि मतं स्वात्मलब्धौ न
[चान्यत् ॥ ३९ ॥

In deep sleep, fire, the sun and others *
are merged in the medial life (madhya
prana) †) which is their source, and
speech and others in the life-breath.
Therefore, is it declared that the cessation is of these senses and not of the
breath. The appearance of objects
through those senses (in the waking state)
is known to be an illusion, like that of
silver in the mother-of-pearl. The
practice of the control of life-forces
enunciated in the Vedanta is therefore
the only means of realising one's own
self and not any other. ‡   (39)

---

*The presiding deities of the senses.

† Another name for virat, primordial substance.

‡ Such as the pandering to the senses or making
them more acute or active.

नो कस्मादार्द्रेमेधः स्पृशति च दहनः किन्तु शुष्कं
                                [निदाघात्
आर्द्रं चेतोऽनुबन्धैः कृतसुकृतमपि स्वोक्तकर्मप्रजार्थैः ।
तद्ज्ज्ञानाग्निरेतत्पृशति न सहता किन्तु वैराग्यशुष्कं
तस्माच्छुद्धो विरागः प्रथममभिहितस्तेन विज्ञान-
                                [सिद्धिः ॥ ४० ॥

Fire does not touch wet fuel even
exceptionally, but only fuel that has been
dried in the sun. So, too, the fire of
knowledge does not touch the mind that
is wet with attachments although it has
acquired merit by the performance of
prescribed duties, the preservation of
progeny and gifts of wealth, but only the
mind that is dried by non-attachment.
Therefore is pure non-attachment taught
foremost, for, by it is the success of
realisation.   (40)

यत्किंचिन्नामरूपात्मकमिदमसदेवोदितं भाति भूमौ
येनानेकप्रकारैर्व्यवहरति जगदेन तेनेश्वरेण ।
तद्वत्प्रच्छादनीयं निभृतरशनया यद्वदेष द्विजिह्वः
तेन त्यक्तेन भोज्यं सुखमनतिशयं मा गृधोऽन्यद्व-
                                [नाद्यम् ॥ ४१ ॥

Whatever is of the nature of name and
form, whatever moves in this world,
springs up as a mere unreality and should

be veiled off by the Lord by whom it is
manifest and by whom it is multifariously
active, in the same way as the (illusory)
snake is veiled off by the rope that is
definitely known. (Only) by abandoning
that (unreality) can unsurpassed bliss be
enjoyed. Do not therefore covet any
other thing like wealth, etc.   (41)

जीवन्मुक्ति मुमुक्षोः प्रथममथ तता मुक्तिरायन्तिकी च
तेऽभ्याससज्ञानयोगाद्रुरुचरणकृपापाङ्गसज्ञेन लब्धात् ।
अभ्यासोऽपि द्विधा स्यादधिकरणवशादैहिको मानसश्च
शारीरस्त्वासनाद्यो ह्युपरितरपरो ज्ञानयोगः पुरोक्तः ॥

To the aspirant for liberation there
first, comes liberation while living and
then ultimate liberation. These two are
the result of constant practice and realisation, which are only attainable by the
contact of the teacher's feet and his
merciful glance. Practice, too, is of two
kinds according to qualification, namely,
bodily and mental. Bodily practice consists of postures (*asanas*), etc., while the
other, previously explained as the path
of knowledge, consists of abstention
(*uparati*).   (42)

सर्वानुन्मूल्य कामान् हृदि कृतनिलयान्क्षिप्तशङ्कुनिवोचैः
दीर्येद्देहाभिमानस्त्यजति चपलतामात्मदत्ताभिमानः ।
यात्यूर्ध्वस्थानमुच्चैः कृतसुकृतभरो नाडिकाभिर्विचित्रैं
नीलश्वेतारुणाभिः स्त्रवदमृतभरं गृह्यमाणात्मसौख्यः ॥

Having rooted out all desires abiding
in the heart as if their pegs were forcibly
broken, he loses all attachment to the
body and gives up his waywardness, his
attention being wholly given to the self.
Then will he of accumulated merit reach
the highest abode* which is variegated
by dark, white and red veins† and wherein ambrosia flows in plenty, and enjoy
the bliss of the self.   (43)

प्रापश्यद्विश्रमात्मेत्ययमिह पुरुषः शोकमोहाद्यतीतः
शुक्रं ब्रह्माध्यगच्छत्स खलु सकलवित्सर्ववसिद्धास्पदं हि ।
विस्मृत्य स्थूलसूक्ष्मप्रभृतिवपुरसौ सर्वसंकल्पशून्यो
जीवन्मुक्तस्तुरीयं पदमधिगतवान्पुण्यपापैर्विहीनः ४४

Such a person, while in this body,
passes beyond sorrow, ignorance and

---

* The thousand-petalled plexus of the *yogins.*

† *Nadi* literally means a tube or vein, but there is
no exact English equivalent for the word as used in
yoga.

other impediments and sees the universe
as the self.* He then attains the shining
Brahman † and becomes all-knowing and
the repository of all occult powers. Afterwards, losing all sense of the gross, subtle and other bodies and devoid of all
volition, he attains the fourth state,‡ and,
purged of all merit and demerit, attains
liberation even in this life. §   **(44)**

यत्सत्त्वाकारवृत्तौ प्रतिफलति युवा देहमात्रावृतोऽपि
तद्धर्मैर्बाल्यवाद्धर्यादिभिरनुपहतः प्राण आविर्बभूव ।
श्रेयान्साध्यस्तमेतं सुनिपुणमतयः सत्यसंकल्पभाजो
ह्यभ्यासादेवयन्तः परिणतमनसा साकमूर्ध्वं नयन्ति ॥

As a result of such realisation of the
self, there springs up the youthful life ‖
which, although encased in a body and
the senses, is unaffected by boyhood, old
age and other bodily attributes, and is

---

* And not as the external universe.
† *Hiranyagarbha.*
‡ The state beyond waking, dream and sleep.
§ *Jivanmukti.*
‖ The *mukhya-prana* or chief breath as distinguished
from the five life-breaths, *prana. apana, vyana, udane*
and *samana.*

extremely blissful and capable of accomplishing the highest goal. It is this life* that is led up,† along with the purified consciousness, by those of supreme wisdom and unfailing resolution, who seek to become divine by spiritual practices. (45)

प्रायोऽकामोऽस्तकामो निरतिशयसुखायात्मकाम-
[स्तदाऽसौ

तत्प्राप्तावाप्तकामः स्थितचरमदशस्तस्य देहावसाने ।
प्राणा नैवोत्क्रमन्ति क्रमविरतिमिताः स्वस्वहेतौ तदानीं
कायं जीवो विलीनो लवणमिव जलेऽखण्ड आत्मैव
[पश्चात् ॥ ४६ ॥

Such a one is almost without desire, for temptations have lost all power over him. He pants only for the realisation of the self for the sake of its unsurpassed bliss. When he realises the self, he has attained all his desires,‡ and remains in the final condition. § When the body dies, the life-breaths do not rise therefrom, ‖ but are gradually dissolved in

* Prana.
† To the thousand-petalled plexus.
‡ He wants nothing else.
§ The fourth state.
‖ The rising is only in case of future birth.

their respective causes. Then, where
will the individual soul be, for it will be
merged, like salt in water, and is then
the Infinite Self itself?   (46)

पिण्डीभूतं यदन्तर्जलनिधिसलिलं याति तत्सैन्धवाख्यं
भूयः प्रक्षिप्तमस्मिन्विलयमुपगतं नामरूपे जहाति ।
प्राज्ञस्तद्द्वत्परात्मन्यथ भजति लयं तस्य चेतो हिमांशौ
वागग्नौ चक्षुरर्कें पयसि पुनरसृगेतसी दिक्षु कर्णौ ॥

Water taken from the sea, when solidi-
fied, goes by the name of salt. When it
is thrown back into the sea and is dissolved, it loses its name and form. So
does the individual soul merge into the
Supreme Self. At the same time, speech
into fire, sight into the sun, blood and
semen into water and hearing into the
directions.   (47)

क्षीरान्तर्यद्वद्दाज्यं मधुरिमविदितं तत्पृथग्भूतमस्मात्
भूतेषु ब्रह्म तद्द्व्यवहृतिविदितं शान्तविश्रान्तिबीजम् ।
यं लब्ध्वा लाभमन्यं तृणमिव मनुते यत्र नोदेति भीतिः
सान्द्रानन्दं यदन्तः स्फुरति तदमृतं विद्धि यतो ह्यन्य-
[दार्तम् ॥ ४८ ॥

Just as butter is contained in milk as
indicated by the sweetness of the latter.

but (when extracted) becomes separate
therefrom, so too is Brahman in every
being as indicated by the activity of the
being. This (Brahman) is the cause of rest
when one is tired.* Attaining it, one
discards all other gain as straw. Therein
springs up no fear. The concentrated
bliss which thus glows within oneself is
immortality. All else is transient. (48)

ओतः प्रोतश्च तन्तुष्विह् विततपटश्चित्रत्रवर्णेषु चित्रः
तस्मिञ्ज्ञिज्ञास्यमाने ननु भवति पटः सूत्रमात्रावशेषः ।
तद्वद्विश्वं विचित्रं नगनगरनरग्राममश्वादिरूपं
प्रोतं वैराजरूपे स वियति तदपि ब्रह्मणि प्रोतमोतम् ॥

The many-coloured cloth is woven-
cross-wise and lengthwise, of threads of
many colours. When this is understood,
there remains nothing of the cloth but
the threads. So is the manifold universe,
with its mountains, cities, men, villages,
beasts, etc., pervaded through and
through, dy the primordial substance,†
that again by æther, and the latter by
Brahman. (49)

---

*E.g., during sleep.   † Virat.

रूपं रूपं प्रतीदं प्रतिफलनवशात्प्रातिरूप्यं प्रपेदे
ह्येको द्रष्टा द्वितीयो भवति च सलिले सर्वतोऽनन्तरूपः ।
इन्द्रो मायाभिरास्ते श्रुतिरिति वदति व्यापकं ब्रह्म
[तस्मात्
जीवत्वं यायकस्मादतिविमलतरे बिम्बितं बुद्ध्युपाधौ ॥

This (Brahman), by virtue of its reflection by various objects,* assumes the various corresponding forms, in the same way as the one seer produces a second one (by reeflction) in water. The Veda too speaks thus of the all-pervading Brahman : "The resplendent one with its powers of illusion, has infinite forms on all sides." The Brahman, therefore, becomes the individual soul by its accidental reflection in the extremely clear consciousness. (50)

तज्ज्ञाः पश्यन्ति बुद्ध्या परमबलवतो माययाऽऽकं पतङ्गं
बुद्धावन्तः समुद्रे प्रतिफलितमरीच्यास्पदं वेधसस्तम् ।
याद्ग्यावानुपाधिः प्रतिफलति तथा ब्रह्म तस्मिन्य-
[थाऽऽस्यं
प्राप्तादर्शानुरूपं प्रतिफलति यथावस्थितं सत्सदैव ॥

The knowers of the self discover, by their wisdom, that the individual soul,†

---

* Technically, *upadhis* or conditions.

† Called here *patanga*, because it eventually falls away.

besmeared by illusion, is only a ray of
the omnipotent Supreme Self reflected in
the ocean of consciousness. This Brahman is variously reflected in accordance
with the form and measure of the medium
reflecting it, in the same way that the
face is variously reflected corresponding
to the mirror in hand ; but it is at all
times what it ever is.*   (51)

एको भानुस्तटस्थः प्रतिफलनवशाद्यस्त्वनेकोदकान्तः
नानात्वं यात्युपाधिस्थितिगतिसमतां चापि तद्वत्परात्मा।
भूतेषूच्चावचेषु प्रतिफलित इवाभाति तावत्स्वभावा-
वच्छिन्नो यः परं तु स्फुटमनुपहतो भाति तावत्स्वभावैः॥

Just as the one sun, independent of
other objects, yet, by virtue of reflection
in several waters, becomes† many and has
the same stability or motion as the
medium reflecting it ; so does the Supreme Self seem to be affected by proper-
ties‡ by virtue of its reflection in all

---

* Just as the face remains the same, whatever the
number and variety of its reflections.
† *i.e'*, seems to become.
‡ Of things and individuals.

beings, high and low, but, when clearly
realised, shines unaffected by those properties.   (52)

यद्वत्पीयूषरश्मौ दिनकरकिरणैर्बिम्बितैरेति सान्द्रं
नाशं नैशं तमिस्रं गृहगतमथवा मूर्च्छितैः कांस्यपात्रे ।
तद्वद्बुद्धौ परात्मद्युतिभिरनुपदं बिम्बिताभिः समन्तात्
भासन्ते हीन्द्रियास्यप्रसृतिभिरनिशं रूपमुख्याः:-

[पदार्थाः ॥ ५३ ॥

Just as the rays of the sun reflected by
the moon or focussed by a mettallic re-
flector dispel the utter darkness of the
night or of the (interior of the) house as
the case may be, so do the rays of the
Supreme Self reflected by the consciousness and streaming forth through the
outlets of the senses, immediately reveal
to us the objects of perception around us,
such as forms etc.   (53)

पूर्णात्मानात्मभेदात् त्रिविधमिह परं बुद्ध्यवच्छिन्न-

[मन्यत्

तत्रैवाभासमात्रं गगनमिव जले त्रिप्रकारं विभाति ।
अम्भोवच्छिन्नमस्मिन्प्रतिफलितमतः पाथसोऽन्तर्बहिश्च
पूर्णावच्छिन्नयोगे व्रजति लयमविद्या स्वकायैं सहैव ॥

The Supreme Self has three aspects,
namely, the full, the self and the not-self,
the first being the unconditioned Self,

the second being that which is conditioned* by the conciousness, and the third being a mere reflection, in the same way as space has three aspects in respect of water, namely, that which is (every where) inside and outside of the water, that which is conterminous with the water, and that which is reflected therein. When the conditioned self is merged in the unconditioned, then the condition† together with its consequences‡ vanishes altogether.   (54)

दृश्यन्ते दारुनार्यो युगपदगणिताः स्तम्भसूत्रप्रयुक्ताः
सङ्गीतं दर्शयन्त्यो व्यवहृतिमपरां लोकसिद्धां च
[सर्वाम् ।

सर्वत्रानुप्रविष्टादभिनवविभवाद्यावदर्थानुबन्धात्
तद्वत्सूत्रात्मसंज्ञाद्व्यवहरति जगद्ब्रूभु र्वस्वर्महान्तम् ॥

Just as countless wooden figures of women, acted upon by means of posts and strings, simultaneously exhibit music and all other activities of common occurrence,§ so does the world, including the regions of *bhur, bhuvar, svar* and *mahar*, carry on all its activities by the inspira-

---

* Or differentiated.   † *Lit*: Nescience.
‡ The reflection, etc.   § In a puppet show.

tion of what is known as the *sutra-atman**
which pervades everything, whose po-
tency is unique and whose inspiration is
in proportion to the end to be achieved.
(55)

तत्सत्यं यत्त्रिकालेष्वनुपहतमदः प्राणदिग्व्योममुख्यं
यस्मिन्विश्रान्तमास्ते तदिह निगदितं ब्रह्म सत्यस्य
                                        [सत्यम् ।
नास्त्यन्यत्किञ्च यद्वत्परमधिकमतो नाम सत्यस्य सत्यं
सच्च त्यच्चेति मूर्तांद्युपहितमवरं सत्यमस्यापि सत्यम् ॥

That is real which is unaffected at all
times.† Such are the unembodied things
like life, space, ether. Even these ultimately resolve themselves‡ into Brahman;
hence is Brahman the reality of the real.
There is naught else which excels it in
its transcendentality or its infinitude;
therefore is it termed the reality of the
real. The lower § that is conditioned by
embodied and unembodied things is
called *satya*, ‖ because it is both *sat* and
tyat.¶ Of this too, Brahman is the reality.
(56)

---

* The thread-self, *i e.*, the self that pervades all, as a
thread running through beads.

† Past, present and future.   ‡ *Lit :* Repose.

§ The individual self, viewed singly or generally.

‖ Real.   ¶ *I.e.*, embodied and disembodied.

यत्किञ्चिद्व्वावसत्यं व्यवहृत्तिविषये रौप्यसर्पाम्बुमुख्यं
तद्वै सत्याश्रयेणेत्ययमिह नियमः सावधिर्लोकसिद्धः ।
तद्वत्सत्यस्य सत्ये जगदखिलमिदं ब्रह्मणि प्राविरासीत्
मिथ्याभूतं प्रतीतं भवति खलु यतस्तच्च सत्यं वदन्ति ॥

Whatever unreal thing is, in every-day
experience, perceived, like silver (in
mother-of-pearl), serpent (in rope) and
water (in mirage), depends for its perception on the real. This rule, with its
limitation, is well-established. So has
this whole universe sprung into existence
in† Brahman, the reality of the real. That
too is called the real by virtue of which
the unreal becomes an object of percep-
tion.   (57)

यत्राकाशावकाशः कलयति च कलामात्रतां यत्र कालो
यत्रैवाशाशवसानं बृहदिह हि विराट् पूर्वमर्वाग्विवास्ते ।
सूत्रं यत्राविरासीन्महदपि महतस्तद्धि पूर्णाञ्च पूर्णं
संपूर्णादर्णवादेरपि भवति यथा पूर्णमेकार्णवाम्भः ५८

---

* That the perception of the unreal is illusory and
ceases when the real object is seen.

† Dependent on Brahman; with Brahman as the
substrate.

The material Brahman,* known as *virat*, is such that the expanse of space, time, and the farthest extremities of the directions, are but infinitesimal parts thereof, and yet it appears to be so close at hand and face to face. From that arose the *sutra-atman*,† greater than the great, fuller than the full, in the same way as the commingled water of the (seven) oceans ‡ is fuller than the full ocean, etc.§   (58)

अन्तः सर्वौषधीनां पृथगमितरसैर्गन्धवैर्यैर्विपाकैः
एकं पाथोदपाथः परिणमति यथा तद्वदेवान्तरात्मा ।
नानाभूतस्वभावैर्वहति वसुमती येन विश्वं पयोदो
वर्षत्युच्चैर्हुंहुताशः पचति दहति वा येन सर्वान्तरोऽसौ ॥

Just as the one rain-water inside all herbs is transformed variously according to the numberless tastes, odours, properties and effects of the respective herbs,

---

* Matter viewed universally, primordial matter.

† The thread-self, otherwise known as *hiranya-garbha*.

‡ At the deluge.

§ The fullness of the diluvial waters is greater than that of the ocean, river, lake, etc., at ordinary times.

so is the inner self* according to the characteristics of the various kinds of beings. By (virtue of) it does the earth support all creatures, the clouds rain profusely, fire cooks and burns. Hence is that the inner (self) of all. (59)

भूतेष्वात्मानमात्मन्यनुगतमखिलं भूतजातं प्रपश्येत्
प्रायः पाथस्तरङ्गान्वयवदथ चिरं सर्वमात्मैव पश्येत् !
एकं ब्रह्माद्वितीयं श्रुतिशिरसि मतं नेह नानाऽस्ति
[किञ्चित्
मृत्योराप्नोति मृत्युं स इह जगदिदं यस्तु नानेव पश्येत्॥

One should clearly realise the self in all beings and all successive multitudes of created beings in the self. He should, repeatedly and persistently, perceive all things as the self, having, for an example the relation between water and waves.† There is only one Brahman without a second, as is declared by the Vedanta. The many do not in any way exist. But he who sees this universe as manifold passes from death to death.‡ (60)

---

* The self in all beings.

† The water and the waves are identical with one another.

‡ *i.e.*, will not attain liberation.

प्राक्पश्चादस्ति कुम्भाद्रगनमिदमिति प्रत्यये सत्यपीदं
कुम्भोत्पत्तावुदेति प्रलयमुपगते नश्यतीलन्यदेशम् ।
नीते कुम्भेन साकं व्रजति भजति वा तत्प्रमाणानुकारौ
इत्थं मिथ्याप्रतीतिःस्फुरति तनुभृतां विश्ववत्सद्दातात्मा ।।

In spite of the knowledge that the
atmosphere exists all around the pot,
there arises in men the false impression
that it has its origin along with the pot,
disappears when the pot is broken, moves
with the pot when it is removed elsewhere, and assumes the same size and
shape as the pot. So is the self in respect of the universe.   (61)

यावान्पिण्डो गुडस्य स्फुरति मधुरिमैवास्ति सर्वोऽपि
                                           [तावान्
यावान्कर्पूरपिण्डः परिणमति सदामोद एवात्र तावान् ।
विश्वं यावद्विभाति द्रुमनगनगरारामचैत्याभिरामं
तावच्चैतन्यमेकं प्रविकसति यतोऽन्ते तदात्मावशेषम् ।।

As much as is a lump of sugar, so much
is nothing but sweetness. As much as a
piece of camphor melts, so much is nothing but sweet fragrance. So, too, as far
as the universe is manifest, with all the
beauty of trees, mountains, cities, gardens
and temples, so far does the one (pure)

consciousness shine forth, for, in the end
all that remains of the universe is the
self.   (62)

वाद्याश्रादानुभूतिर्यदपि तदपि सा नूनमाघातगम्या
वाद्याघातध्वनीनां न पृथगनुभवः किन्तु तत्साहचर्यात् ।
मायोपादानमेतत्सहचरितमिव ब्रह्मणाऽऽभाति तद्वत्
तस्मिन्प्रत्यक्प्रतीते न किमपि विषयीभावमाप्नोति
                                      [यस्मात् ॥ ६३ ॥

Although the hearing of the sound
proceeds from the musical instrument, it
is nevertheless produced only by striking
the instrument. The sounds that proceed
from striking the instrument are not
heard separately but only in conjunction
with the striking. So, too, this universe,
whose efficient cause is illusion (*maya*), is
manifest, as it were, in conjunction with
Brahman. But when that Brahman is inwardly realised, nothing will remain the
object of perception.   (63)

दृष्टः साक्षादिदानीमिह खलु जगतामीश्वरः संविदात्मा
विज्ञानस्थाणुरेको गगनवदभितः सर्वभूतान्तरात्मा ।
दृष्टं ब्रह्मातिरिक्तं सकलमिदमसद्रूपमाभासमात्रं
शुद्धं ब्रह्माहमस्मीत्यविरतमधुनाऽनैव तिष्ठेदनीहः॥६४॥

It is thus clearly seen that the Lord of all
the worlds is of the nature of pure consci-

ousness is the one Immovable that is
knowledge itself, is all-pervading like
ether, and is the inner spirit of all beings.
It is also seen that all this universe is
different from Brahman, is unreal by
nature, and is a mere semblance. One
should, therefore, even now and here,
give up all desires and remain for ever
fixed in the thought "I am Brahman."
(64)

इन्द्रेन्द्राण्योः प्रकामं सुरतसुखजुषोः स्वाद्रतान्तः सुषुप्तिः
तस्यामानन्दसान्द्रं पदमतिगहनं यत्स आनन्दकोशः ।
तस्मिन्नो वेद किञ्चिन्निरतिशयसुखाभ्यन्तरे लीयमानो
दुःखी स्याद्वोधितः सन्निति कुशलमतिर्बोधयेन्नैव सुप्तम् ॥

When Indra and Indrani have freely enjoyed the bliss of union, the cessation of
their pleasure is deep sleep. * Therein
is a state that is full of concentrated bliss
and very difficult to comprehend; that is
the *anandakosa* (the bliss-sheath). In that

---

  *Indra represents the ' man ' in the right eye and
Indrani the light in the left eye that reveals all things
to our vision. During waking, the two reside between the brows. When they descend into the heart
and enjoy the bliss of union, it is then the dream-state.
When that condition ends, the state of deep sleep
sets in.

condition one is not conscious of anything, being deeply merged in unsurpassed bliss. If awaked, he becomes unhappy. A wise man should therefore
never awake a sleeping person.   (65)

सर्वे नन्दन्ति जीवा अधिगतयशसा गृह्णता चक्षुरादीन्
अन्तः सर्वोपकर्त्रो बहिरपि च सुषुप्तौ यथा तुल्यसंस्थाः ।
एतेषां किल्बिषस्पृग्जठरभृतिकृते यो बहिर्वृत्तिरास्ते
त्वक्चक्षुःश्रोत्रनासारसनवशमितो याति शोकं च
[मोहम् ॥ ६६ ॥

All beings* enjoy bliss by attaining
Brahman (yasas) which embraces within
itself the eye and other sensory organs
and which externally helps all perception.
All individual souls are alike in nature as
in deep sleep.† Among these, he who,
for the sake of feeeding the belly, remains only externally active and is
enslaved by the senses of touch, sight,
hearing, smell and taste, becomes tainted
with sin and suffers misery and confusion.
(66)

---

*Individual souls.
† Devoid of caste, colour, creed, etc.

जाग्रत्यामन्तरात्मा विषयसुखकृतेऽनेकयत्नान्विधास्यन्
श्राम्यत्सर्वेन्द्रियौघोऽधिगतमपि सुखं विसरन्याति
[निद्राम् ।
विश्रामाय स्वरूपे त्वतितरसुलभं तेन चातीन्द्रियं हि
सुखं   सर्वोत्तमं   स्यात्परिणतिविरसादिन्द्रियोत्थात्सु-
[खाच ॥ ६७ ॥

The individual soul, during the waking
state, puts forth innumerable efforts for
the attainment of sensual pleasures, and
when the entire group of sensory organs
is fatigued, it forgets even the pleasure
on hand and goes into sleep, in order
that it may enjoy rest in its own nature.
Ultra-sensual bliss is thus extremely easy
of attainment and is far superior to the
pleasure derived from the senses which
always produces disgust in the end.   (67)

पक्षावभ्यस्य पक्षी जनयति मरुतं तेन यात्युष्वदेशं
लब्ध्वा वायुं महान्तं श्रममपनयति स्वीयपक्षौ प्रसार्य ।
दुःसङ्कल्पैर्विकल्पैर्विषयमनुकदर्थीकृतं चित्तमेतत्
खिन्नं विश्रामहेतोः स्वपिति चिरमहो हस्तपादान्प्रसार्य॥

The bird, by the motion of its wings,
generates a breeze and, by its aid, reaches
a great height, and there, having attained

the vast expanse of the atmosphere, cures
itself of its fatigue by spreading its
wings. So, too, this mind, troubled by
many evil desires and doubts in respect
of objects of pleasure, and fatigued
thereby, stretches forth the hands and
sleeps long for the sake of rest. (68)

आश्लिष्यात्मानमात्मा न किमपि सहसैवान्तरं वेद बाह्यं
यद्वत्कामी विदेशात्सदनमुपगतो गाढमाश्लिष्य
[कान्ताम् ।

यात्यस्तं तत्र लोकव्यवहृतिरखिला पुण्यपापानुबन्ध:
शोको मोहो भयं वा समविषममिदं न स्मरत्येव
[किञ्चित् ॥

The moment that the individual soul
comes into union with the self (Brahman),
it ceases to be conscious of anything,
internal, or external like unto a lover
fervently embracing his beloved one on
his return home from a foreign land. In
that state all worldly activity that is the
result of merit and demerit, disappears,
and nothing is remembered of all these
ups and downs,—sorrow, confusion, or
fear. (69)

---

*During deep sleep.

अल्पानल्पप्रपञ्चप्रलय उपरतिश्चेन्द्रियाणां सुखाप्तिः
जीवन्मुक्तौ सुषुप्तौ त्रितयमपि समं किन्तु तत्रास्ति भेदः ।
प्राक्संस्कारात्प्रसुप्तः पुनरपि च पुरावृत्तिमेति प्रबुद्धो
नश्यत्संस्कारजातो न स किल पुनरावर्तते यश्च मुक्तः ॥

The disappearance of all gross and
subtle existence, the cessation of the
senses, and the attainment of bliss,—
these three are common to liberation-
while alive and deep sleep.   There is
however this difference that, whereas he
who is asleep comes back to life again
and again* by virtue of the effects of his
past actions, he that has attained illumi-
nation and liberation, never comes back
(to worldly life), because the effects of all
his past actions have been destroyed.

(70)

आनन्दान्यश्च सर्वाननुभवति नृपः सर्वसंपत्समृद्धः
तस्यानन्दः स एकः स खलु शतगुणः संप्रदिष्टः
                                        [पितृणाम् ।
आदेवब्रह्मलोकं शतशतगुणितास्ते यदन्तर्गताः स्युः
ब्रह्मानन्दः स एकोऽस्त्यथ विषयसुखान्यस्य मात्रा
                                        [भवन्ति ॥ ७१ ॥

If the bliss of a king endowed with all
prosperity and enjoying every kind of

---

*Passes through births and deaths.

happiness be taken as a unit, the bliss of
the *manes* is declared to be a hundredfold.
So, too, through the world of the gods
higher and higher up to the world of
Brahman, each (bliss) is a hundredfold of
the next lower one. Singular and con-
taining within itself all these (grades of
bliss) is the bliss of (the supreme) Brahman, of which the pleasures of the senses
are but an (insignificant) fraction.   (71)

यत्रानन्दाश्च मोदाः प्रमुद इति मुदश्चासते सर्वे एते
यत्राप्ताः सर्वकामाः स्युरखिलविरमात्केवलीभाव
[आस्ते ।

मां तत्रानन्दसान्द्रे कृधि चिरममृतं सोम पीयूषपूर्णां
धारामिन्द्राय देहीत्यपि निगमगिरो भ्रूयुगान्तर्गताय ॥

" Therein are included all degrees of
bliss,—the bliss of men (*ananda*), of the
manes (*moda*), of gods (*pramoda*), etc.
Therein all desires are fulfilled. Therein
is the state of oneness owing to the
cessation of all (phenomena). Make me
live immortally for ever, O Soma,* in that
abode of concentrated bliss, and vouch-
safe to my soul † that is betwixt the

---

* Lit. the moon. Here " *hiranyagarbha*."
† ' Indra ' in the text.

brows an unceasing shower of immortality,* "—so do the Vedas declare.   (72)

आत्माऽकम्पः सुखात्मा स्फुरति तदपरा त्वन्यथैव

[स्फुरन्ती

स्थैर्यं वा चञ्चलत्वं मनसि परिणतिं याति तत्रत्वमस्मिन्।

चाञ्चल्यं दुःखहेतुर्मनस इदमहो यावदिष्टार्थलब्धिः

तस्यां यावत्स्थिरत्वं मनसि विषयजं स्यात्सुखं तावदेव॥

The self is unperturbed and its nature
is bliss; the other (*maya*) is quite the
opposite; their steadinees or perturbation
bears fruit in the individual consciousness.   The perturbation of the mind,
until a desired object is gained, gives rise
to misery. When that object is gained
the pleasure (said to be) derived from
that object is only so long as the mind
remains steady.   (73)

यद्वत्सौख्यं रतान्ते निमिषमिह मनस्येकताने रसे स्यात्

स्थैर्यं यावत्सुषुप्तौ सुखमनतिशयं तावदेवाथ मुक्तौ ।

नित्यानन्दः प्रशान्ते हृदि तदिह सुखस्थैर्ययोः साहचर्यं

नित्यानन्दस्य मात्रा विषयसुखमिदं युज्यते तेन

[वक्तुम् ॥ ७४ ॥

Just as there is a momentary bliss when
the mind is absorbed in pleasure at the

___
*Lit. nectar.

end of a sensual indulgence, so too there
is unsurpassed bliss in deep sleep only
so long as there is steadiness (of consciousness).   In liberation, however, the
consciousness is absolutely tranquil and
there is eternal bliss.   There is thus a
constant relation between bliss and steadiness.   It is therefore proper to speak of
sensual pleasure as a fraction of eternal
bliss.   (74)

श्रान्तं स्वान्तं सबाह्यव्यवहृतिभिरिदं ताः समाकृष्य

[सर्वाः

तत्तत्संस्कारयुक्तं ह्युपरमति परावृत्तमिच्छन्निदानम् ।

स्वाप्नान्संस्कारजातप्रजनितविषयान्स्वाप्रदेहेऽनुभूतान्

प्रोज्झ्यान्तः प्रत्यगात्मप्रवणमिदमगाद्धूरि विश्रामम-

[स्मिन् ॥ ७५ ॥

The mind, tired of external activities,
draws them all in together, and carrying
with it the tendencies resulting from
them, ceases from them and turns inward
in search of its own place.   In the dream-
body, it enjoys dream-objects generated
by the combination of those tendencies.
Abandoning these, again, it longs for the
inner self, reaching which it attains
perfect rest.*   (75)

_____

*Tranquillity, bliss.

स्वप्ने भोगः सुखादेर्भवति ननु कुतः साधने मूर्च्छेमाने
स्वाप्नं देहान्तरं तद्व्यवहृतिकुशलं नव्यमुत्पद्यते चेत् ।
तत्सामग्र्या अभावात्कुत इदमुदितं तद्धि सांकल्पिकं
                                          [चेत्

तर्कि स्वप्ने रतान्ते वपुषि निपतिते दृश्यते रक्तमोक्षः ॥

*" How is the enjoyment of pleasure,
etc. possible in dream, while the instrument therefor (the gross body) is inert?
If (it be said that) a new dream body fit
for such activity springs up, wherefrom
does it arise, since the means of its gene-
ration † is absent? If it be a product of
the imagination, then how is it that, after
the experience of sexual pleasure in a
dream, the effect thereof is (actually)
visible in the body that is inert?   (76)

भीत्या रोदित्यनेन प्रवदति हसति श्लाघते नूनमस्मात्
स्वप्नेऽप्यङ्गेऽनुबन्धं त्यजति न सहसा मूर्च्छितोऽप्यन्त-
                                          [रात्मा ।

पूर्वं ये येऽनुभूतास्तनुयुवतिह्यव्याघ्रदेशादयोऽर्थाः
तत्संस्कारस्वरूपान्सृजति पुनरमूनिश्रित्य संस्कारदेहम् ॥

" It is with this (the gross body) that he
weeps from fear, talks, laughs and

---

*This and part of the next verse are the arguments
of an opponent.

† Such as parents.

exults." It surely follows from this that the inner self does not abruptly sever its connection with the body during dream, although that body is inert ; but, with the help of the subtle body, it creates again, in subtle form, those objects which it had previously † experienced, such as the body, woman, horse, tiger, locality, etc. (77)

सन्धौ जाग्रत्सुषुप्त्योरनुभवविदितास्वाप्न्यवस्था द्वितीया
तत्रात्मज्योतिरास्ते पुरुष इह समाकृष्य सर्वेन्द्रियाणि ।
संवेश्य स्थूलदेहं समुचितशयने स्वीयभासाऽन्तरात्मा
पश्यन्संस्काररूपानभिमतविषयान्याति कुत्रापि तद्वत् ॥

The second state, that of dream, is known by experience to be midway between waking and sleep. In that state the individual, having withdrawn all the senses, has only the light of the self remaining. The gross body having been laid down on a suitable bed, the inner self, experiencing the objects it likes in their subtle form, goes about as it pleases in the same manner.‡ (78)

---

*This is the answer to the opponent.
† In the waking state.   ‡ With the subtle body.

रक्षन्प्राणैः कुलायं निजशयनगतं श्वासमात्रावशेषैः
माभूत्तत्प्रेतकल्पाकृतिकमिति पुनः सारमेयादिभक्ष्यम् ।
स्वप्ने स्वीयप्रभावात्सृजति ह्यरथान्निम्नगाः पल्वलानि
क्रीडास्थानान्यनेकान्यपि सुहृद्बलापुत्रमित्रानुकारान् ॥

Preserving the body lying in bed by
means of the life-forces now reduced to
mere breath, lest it assume the form of a
corpse and become food for dogs, etc., it
creates, in dream, by its own power,
horses, chariots, rivers, pounds, play-
grounds, companions, women, sons,
friends,—all by way of imitation.† (79)

मातङ्गव्याघ्रदस्युद्विषद्दुर्गकपीन् कुत्रचित्प्रेयसीभिः
क्रीडन्नास्ते हसन्वा विहरति कुहचिन्मृष्टमश्नाति चान्नम् ।
म्लेच्छत्वं प्राप्तवानस्म्यहमिति कुहचिच्छङ्कितः स्वीय-
[लोकान्

आस्ते व्याघ्रादिभीत्या प्रचलति कुहचिद्रोदिति
[प्रस्यमानः ॥ ८० ॥

It creates elephants, tigers, robbers,
enemies, snakes and monkeys. Sometimes it is playing with beloved damsels.
Sometimes it laughs and sports. Some-

---

† Of its waking experiences.

times it eats delicious food. At other
times it is afraid of its kith and kin, because it has become an outcaste.   And at
other times it runs away for fear of tigers
etc. or is caught by them and wails. (80)

योयो दृग्गोचरोऽर्थो भवति सस तदा तद्द्वृतात्मखरूपा-
विज्ञानोतपद्यमानः स्फुरति ननु यथा शुक्तिकाऽज्ञानहेतुः ।
रौप्याभासो मृषैव स्फुरति च किरणाज्ञानतोऽम्भो
                                        [भुजङ्गो
रज्ज्वज्ञानान्निमेषं सुखभयकृदतो दृष्टिसृष्टं किलेदम् ॥

Whatever object is perceived, it comes
into existence then and there by the ignorance of the true nature of the self that is
in it. Its manifestation is like the unreal
appearance of false silver owing to one's
not recognising the mother-of-pearl, or
of the mirage owing to one's not recognising the sun's rays, or of the serpent
by one's not recognising the rope,—such
appearance giving rise to joy or fear,
only for an   instant. Hence all this
universe is really created by perception.†
                                        (81)

---

† That is, the existence of any object is only so long
and so much as we perceive it.

मायाध्यासाश्रयेण प्रविततमखिलं यन्मया तेन मत्स्था-
न्येतान्येतेषु नाहं यदपि हि रजतं भाति शुक्तौ न रौप्ये ।
शुक्त्यंशस्तेन भूतान्यपि मयि न वसन्तीति विश्वग्वि-
                                                   [नेता

प्राहास्माइश्यजातं सकलमपि मृषैवेन्द्रजालोपमेयम् ॥

The Lord of the Universe has declared ; "By me, on whom depends the illusion of *maya*, all this (universe) has been
spread forth. Therefore, all things are in
me, not I in them; for instance, although
silver appears (falsely) in the mother-o'-
pearl, there is naught of the mother-o'-
pearl in silver. Therefore, †too, all
things do not (in reality) exist in me."
It follows from this that the whole objective world is as unreal as the products of
jugglery.   (82)

हेतुः कर्मैव लोके सुखतदितरयोरेवमज्ञोऽविदित्वा
मित्रं वा शत्रुरित्थं व्यवहरति मृषा याज्ञवल्क्यार्ते-
                                                   [भागौ ।
यत्कर्मैवोचतुः प्राग्जनकनृपगृहे चक्रतुस्तत्प्रशंसां
वंशोत्तंसो यदूनामिति वदति न कोऽप्यत्र तिष्ठत्यकर्मा ॥

Action is the only cause of happiness
or misery in this world. The ignorant,

---

† Because the universe is the creation of *maya*.

not knowing this, speak in vain of friend or enemy.* Yagnavalkya and A'rtabhaga, of yore, in the palace of king Janaka, spoke only of action and praised it. Even the ornament † of the race of Yadu declares: "None in this world remains without action." (83)

वृक्षच्छेदे कुठारः प्रभवति यदपि प्राणिनोद्यस्तथाऽपि
प्रायोऽन्नं तृप्तिहेतुस्तदपि निगदितं कारणं भोक्तृयत्नः ।
प्राचीनं कर्म तद्द्विषमसमफलप्राप्तिहेतुस्तथाऽपि
स्वातन्त्र्यं नश्वरेऽस्मिन्न हि खलु घटते प्रेरकोऽस्तान्-
[रात्मा ॥ ८४ ॥

Although the axe is able to fell a tree, it should nevertheless be wielded by a living being. Food is no doubt, a source of satisfaction, but the real cause thereof is the effort ‡ of the eater. In the same way, former action is the cause of the good or evil results experienced, yet, being itself evanescent, it cannot do this by itself, It is impelled thereto by the inner self. (84)

---

*One who gives happiness or one who causes misery.

† Krishna.   ‡ Cooking and eating.

स्मृत्या लोकेषु वर्णाश्रमविहितमदो नित्यकाम्यादि कर्म
सर्वं ब्रह्मार्पणं स्यादिति निगमगिरः संगिरन्तेऽतिरम्यम् ।
यन्त्रासानेत्रजिह्वाकरचरणशिरःश्रोत्रसन्तर्पणेन
तुष्येदङ्गीव साक्षात्तरुरिव सकलो मूलसन्तर्पणेन ॥८५॥

The Vedas declare, with much pro-
priety, that all rites, compulsory, discre-
tionary, and so on, which are laid down
by the Smriti for the various castes and
conditions of men, are (in reality) dedicated to the Supreme Self ; * in the same
way that by the satisfaction of the nose,
eyes, tongue, hands, feet, head and ears,
it is the inner man that is actually satisfied, and, by the watering of the roots of
a tree, every part of that tree is
nourished.   (85)

यःप्रैष्यात्मानभिज्ञः श्रुतिविदपि तथा कर्मकृत्कर्मणोऽस्य
नाशः स्यादल्पभोगात्पुनरवतरणे दुःखभोगो महीयान् ।
आत्माभिज्ञस्य लिप्सोरपि भवति महान्शाश्वतः सिद्धि-
                                    [भोगो
ह्यात्मा तस्मादुपास्यः खलु तदधिगमे सर्वसौख्यान्य-
                                    [लिप्सोः ॥ ८६ ॥

---

*Whatever lesser deity might be invoked in
practice.

After death, he who is ignorant of the self, although versed in the Vedas, and has performed the rites prescribed therein, exhausts his merit after a brief enjoyment and undergoes very great misery in having to be born again. He who has realised the self and yet longs for reward, enjoys much greater and more lasting happiness accompanied by supernatural powers. Therefore, one should indeed realise the self; for, by realising it, one gains every happiness although he longs for no reward. (86)

सूर्यैंदैरर्थमानं न हि भवति पुनः केवलैर्नात्र चित्रं
सूर्योत्सूर्यप्रतीतिर्न भवति सहसा नापि चन्द्रस्य चन्द्रात् ।
अग्नेरग्नेश्च किन्तु स्फुरति रविमुखं चक्षुषश्चित्प्रयुक्तात्
आत्मज्योतिस्ततोऽयं पुरुष इह महो देवतानां च
[चित्रम् ॥ ८७ ॥

It is no wonder that objects are not revealed by the sun, moon, etc., of their own accord; nor is the sun directly perceived by its own light, nor the moon, nor fire. On the other hand, the sun, moon, etc., are perceived by means of the sense of sight inspired by (the inner) consciousness. Therefore, only the dweller in the body shines by his own light. Yet, in the world,† the deities‡ have their respective power to illuminate. (87)

प्राणेनाम्भांसि भूयः पिबति पुनरसावन्नमश्राति तत्र
तत्पाकं जाठरोऽग्निस्तदुपहितबलो द्राक् शनैर्वा करोति ।
व्यानः सर्वाङ्गनाडीष्वथ नयति रसं प्राणसन्तर्पणार्थं
निस्सारं पूतिगन्धं त्यजति बहिरयं देहतोऽपानसंज्ञः ॥

Through the life-force called *prana* the individual drinks plenty of water and eats food. Then the abdominal fire, with energy derived from that (*prana*), digests it sooner or later. Thereafter the life-force known as *vyana* carries the essence along the blood-vessels of the whole body for the nourishment of life; and the life-force termed *apana* expels from the body the putrid non-essence. (88)

---

† *i.e.*, as far as the senses are concerned.

‡ The sun, moon, etc., which preside over the senses. In relation to objects, the senses have power to reveal them, although their light is but a reflection of the resplendence of the self.

व्यापारं देहसंस्थः प्रतिवपुरखिलं पञ्चवृत्त्यात्मकोऽसौ
प्राणः सर्वेन्द्रियाणामधिपतिरनिशं सत्तया निर्विवादम् ।
यस्येत्थं चिद्धनस्य स्फुटमिह कुरुते सोऽस्मि सर्वस्य
[साक्षी
प्राणस्य प्राण एषोऽप्यखिलतनुभृतां चक्षुषश्चक्षुरेषः ॥

This life, with its five-fold energy*,
residing in each body and being master
of all the senses, distinctly and incessantly carries on all the activities appro-
priate to that particular body, by a power
which belongs undoubtedly to the self
that is pure consciousness. That self am
I, the all-seer, the life behind all life, the
consciousness behind the consciousness
of all beings.   (89)

यं भान्तं चिद्धनैकं क्षितिजलपवनादित्यचन्द्रादयो ये
भासा तस्यैव चानु प्रविरलगतयो भान्ति तस्मिन्वसन्ति ।
विद्युत्पुञ्जोऽस्मिसङ्घोऽप्युडुगणवितिर्भासयेत्किं परेशं
ज्योतिःशान्तं ह्यनन्तं कविमजममरं शाश्वतं जन्म-
[शून्यम् ॥ ९० ॥

By the light of that One Self that is
pure consciousness, the earth, water, air,
sun, moon, etc., shine after It, each with
its peculiar characteristics, and   have

---
*Prana, apana, udana, samana, vyana.

their being in It. Can the flashes of
lightning and flaming conflagrations and
the vast expanse of starry galaxies illu-
mine the Supreme Lord, the immutable,
infinite light, the seer, without beginning
and without end, eternal, because devoid
of origin ?   (90)

तद्ब्रह्मैवाहमस्मीत्यनुभव उदितो यस्य कस्यापि चेद्वै
पुंसः श्रीसद्गुरूणामतुलितकरुणापूर्णपीयूषदृष्ट्या ।
जीवन्मुक्तः स एव भ्रमविधुरमना निर्गतेऽनाद्युपाधौ
नित्यानन्दैकधाम प्रविशति परमं नष्टसन्देहवृत्तिः ॥

If, by the favour of the nectar-like
glance, full of unparralleled mercy, of the
venerable holy Master, there arises, in
any man whatsoever, the realisation
" That very Brahman am I," he indeed
loses all feelings of doubt and, with his
mind free from illusion, attains liberation
even while living in the body. (Thereafter), when the beginningless limitation* is completely dissolved, he is merged in the Highest, the sole abode of
eternal bliss.   (91)

*Maya, the root-illusion.

नो देहो नेन्द्रियाणि क्षरमतिचपलं नो मनो नैव बुद्धिः
प्राणो नैवाहमस्मीत्यखिलजडमिदं वस्तुजातं कथं स्याम् ।
नाहंकारो न दारा गृहसुतसुजनक्षेत्रवित्तादि दूरं
साक्षी चित्प्रत्यगात्मा निखिलजगदधिष्ठानभूतः शिवो-
[ऽहम् ॥ ९२ ॥

I am neither the dense body nor the
senses, nor the evanescent and most
erratic mind, nor reason, nor life, nor the
ego, nor wife, nor house, nor offspring,
nor kith and kin, nor land nor wealth,
and so on. For, how, can I, the witness
aloof, the pure consciousness, the inner
self, be all these things which are purely
objective? I am the Supreme* that is the
reality behind all this universe.   (92)

दृश्यं यद्रूपमेतद्द्रवति च विशदं नीलपीताद्यनेकं
सर्वस्यैतस्य दृग्वै स्फुरदनुभवतो लोचनं चैकरूपम् ।
तद्दृश्यं मानसं दृक्परिणतविषयाकारधीवृत्तयोऽपि
दृश्या दृग्रूप एव प्रभुरिह स तथा दृश्यते नैव साक्षी ॥

In relation to all these plainly visible
forms of dark, yellow and other innumerable colours, the eye, which is one, is the

---

Siva, or *parabrahman* considered as *ananda
maya*.

seer, for, therein arises the perception.
The eye, in its turn, is only objective because the mind is its seer.   And even the
workings of the mind, objective forms
transformed into thought, are, in their
turn, objective.   The Lord alone is the
absolute seer, the witness, for, He is
never, like the above, objective.   (93)

रज्ज्वज्ञानाद्भुजङ्गस्तदुपरि सहसा भाति मन्दान्धकारे
स्वात्माज्ञानात्तथाऽसौ   भृशमसुखमभूदात्मनो जीव-
[भावः ।

आप्नोत्त्याऽहिभ्रमान्ते सच खलु विदिता रज्जुरेका
[तथाऽहं

कूटस्थो नैव जीवो निजगुरुवचसा साक्षिभूतः
[शिवोऽहम् ॥ ९४ ॥

Owing to the non-recognition of a rope
in the twilight, over it appears a serpent
all at once.   In the same way is the
extremely unhappy condition of the individual soul imposed on the self by reason
of the non-realisation of one's own
self.   Again, when the illusion of a serpent is dispelled by the admonition of a
trustworthy friend, there is only the old
familiar rope.   So, too, by the admonition of my own Master, I am not the individual soul, but the immutable Self that
is the seer. I am the Supreme Bliss (*Siva*).
(94)

किं ज्योतिस्ते वदस्वाहनि रविरिह मे चन्द्रदीपादि रात्रौ
स्यादेवं भानुदीपादिकपरिकलने किं तव ज्योतिरस्ति ।
चक्षुस्तन्मीलने किं भवति च सुतरां धीर्धियः किं प्रकाशे
तत्रैवाहं ततस्त्वं तदसि परमकं ज्योतिरस्मि प्रभोऽहम् ॥

Tell me what is thy light. You say:
"The sun in the day and the moon,
lamp, etc., at night." It may be so, but
by what light do you see the sun, the
lamp, etc.? You say: "the eye." But
when that is closed, what brighter light
is there? You reply: "the mind." By
what light is the mind revealed? "For
that, I alone am the light," you say. You
are therefore that Supreme Light. "I
am, my Master."
(95)

कश्चित्कालं स्थितः कौ पुनरिह भजते नैव देहादिसंघं
यावत्प्रारब्धभोगं कथमपि स सुखं चेष्टतेऽसङ्गबुद्धया ।
निर्द्वन्द्वो नित्यशुद्धो विगलितममताहङ्कृतिर्नित्यतृप्तो
ब्रह्मानन्दस्वरूपः स्थिरमतिरचलो निर्गताशेषमोहः ॥

Such a one* after remaining on the
earth for a time, never more returns to a
body and its accompaniments; until the

---

*One that has realised "I am Brahman."

enjoyment of the ripe fruits of his former
actions is completed, he lives in a peculiar manner, but blissfully, because his
mind is free from all contrasts,* ever
pure, devoid of my-ness and I-ness,
always contented, identical in nature with
infinite bliss, steady in thought, imperturbable, cleansed of all illusions.†   (96)

जीवात्मब्रह्मभेदं दलयति सहसा यत्प्रकाशैकरूपं
विज्ञानं तच्च बुद्धौ समुदितमतुलं यस्य पुंसः पवित्रम् ।
माया तेनैव तस्य क्षयमुपगमिता संसृतेः कारणं या
नष्टा सा कार्यक त्रीपुनरपि भविता नैव विज्ञानमात्रात् ॥

Such an absolutely resplendent realisation at once destroys the distinction
between the individual soul and Supreme
Self. In whomsoever such an unimpeded
unparalleled- realisation springs up in
consciousness, for him the root-illusion
(maya) that is the source of births and
deaths, is destroyed by that very realisation. Once destroyed, it can no more
create illusions by its power of phenomenal manifestation.   (97)

---

*Happiness and misery, gain and loss, etc.
† This verse describes a *jivan-mukta*.

विश्वं नेति प्रमाणाद्विगलितजगदाकारभानस्त्यजेद्वै
पीत्वा यद्वत्फलाम्भस्त्यजति च सुतरां तत्फलं सौरभा-
[ढ्यम्
सम्यक् सच्चिद्घनैकामृतसुखकबलास्वादपूर्णो हृदाऽसौ
ज्ञात्वा निस्सारमेवं जगदखिलमिदं स्वप्रभः शान्तचित्तः॥

Knowing that the universe is unreal
and having, therefore, completely destroyed all perception of phenomenal
forms, he should taste, to his heart's
utmost content, the morsel of immortal
bliss that is the highest and most perfect
concentration of being and consciousness,
and filled with light of the self and with
a tranquil mind, he should realise that
all this universe is unessential and should
therefore abandon it, in the same way as
one, after drinking the juice of a fruit,
throws it away although the remnant
may be highly fragrant.   (98)

क्षीयन्ते चास्य कर्माण्यपि खलु हृदयग्रन्थिस्तद्धिद्यते वै
छिद्यन्ते संशया ये जनिमृतिफलदा दृष्टमात्रे परेशे ।
तस्मिन्नश्चिन्मात्ररूपे गुणमलरहिते तत्त्वमस्यादिलक्ष्ये
कूटस्थे प्रत्यगात्मन्यखिलविधिमनोऽगोचरे ब्रह्मणीशे ॥

The results of actions are destroyed,
the bondage of the heart is broken,

and all doubts, which lead one to births
and deaths, are removed, as soon as one
realises that Supreme Lord, whose nature
is pure consciousness, who is devoid of
the stain of qualities, who is realisable
by such teachings as " That thou art,"
the immutable inner self, the Brahman,
the Lord, that is beyond all command-
ments and beyond all thought.   (99)

आदौ मध्ये तथाऽन्ते जनिमृतिफलदं कर्ममूलं विशालं
ज्ञात्वा संसारवृक्षं भ्रममदमुदिताशोकतानेकपत्रम् ।
कामक्रोधादिशाखं सुतपशुवनिताकन्यकापक्षिसंघं
छित्वाऽसङ्गासिनैनं पटुमतिरभितश्चिन्तयेद्वासुदेवम् ॥

One should understand the huge tree
of phenomenal existence, which bears
the fruits of births and deaths before,
betwixt and after, whose roots are the
results of past actions, whose countless
leaves are delusions, vanities, joys and
sorrows, whose branches are desire,
anger, etc., and on which dwell the birds
of sons and cattle, wives and daughters,
in large numbers. Such a wise man
should fell this tree down with the axe

of non-attachment and should at all
times meditate upon the Supreme Being
(*Vasudeva*).   (100)

जातं मय्येव सर्वं पुनरपि मयि तत्संस्थितं चैव विश्वं
सर्वं मय्येव याति प्रविलयमिति तद्ब्रह्म चैवाहमस्मि ।
यस्य स्मृत्या च यज्ञाद्यखिलशुभविधौ सुप्रयातीह कार्यं
न्यूनं सम्पूर्णतां वै तमहमतिमुदैवाच्युतं सन्नतोऽस्मि ॥

The whole universe is born in me, has
its support in me and dissolves in me.
Therefore, that very Brahman indeed am
I. Again, humbly and exultingly do I
bow to that Immutable Being (*achyuta*), by
whose mere remembrance defective pro-
cedure in all auspicious acts like sacrifices
is rendered perfectly complete.   (101)

Thus ends the Century of Verses.

॥ इति शतश्लोकी समाप्ता ॥

———

॥ आत्मबोधः ॥

KNOWLEDGE OF SELF

तपोभिः क्षीणपापानां शान्तानां वीतरागिणाम् ।
मुमुक्षूणामपेक्ष्योऽयमात्मबोधो विधीयते ॥ १ ॥

This treatise called "Knowledge of
Self" is written for the sake of those
whose sins have been destroyed by
austerities and who, with a tranquil mind
and free from attachment, long for
liberation. (1)

बोधोऽन्यसाधनेभ्यो हि साक्षान्मोक्षैकसाधनम् ।
पाकस्य वह्निवज्ज्ञानं विना मोक्षो न सिध्यति ॥ २ ॥

Compared with all other means, knowledge is the only direct means to
liberation. As cooking is impossible
without fire, so is liberation impossible
without knowledge. (2)

अविरोधितया कर्म नाविद्यां विनिवर्तयेत् ।
विद्याऽविद्यां निहन्त्येव तेजस्तिमिरसंघवत् ॥ ३ ॥

Ritual cannot dispel ignorance, because
they are not mutually contradictory. But

knowledge surely destroys ignorance, as
light destroys the densest darkness.   (3)

अविच्छिन्न इवाज्ञानात्तन्नाशे सति केवलः ।
स्वयं प्रकाशते ह्यात्मा मेघापायेंऽशुमानिव ।   ॥ ४ ॥

The self appears to be conditioned by
virtue of ignorance. But when that (ignorance) is destroyed, the unconditioned
self shines by its own light, like the sun
when the clouds have disappeared.   (4)

अज्ञानकलुषं जीवं ज्ञानाभ्यासाद्विनिर्मलम् ।
कृत्वा ज्ञानं स्वयं नश्येज्जलं कतकरेणुवत्   ॥ ५ ॥

Having purified, by repeated instruction, the soul that is turbid with
ignorance, knowledge should efface itself,
as the paste of the cleaning-nut does
with water.*   (5)

संसारः स्वप्नतुल्यो हि रागद्वेषादिसंकुलः ।
स्वकाले सत्यवद्भाति प्रबोधेऽसत्यसद्भवेत्   ॥ ६ ॥

The phenomenal world, abounding in
desire, hatred, etc., is verily like a dream.

---

*The cleaning-nut, rubbed into a paste and thrown
into dirty water, clears the water and itself settles
down along the dirt as a sediment,

While it lasts, it seems to be real, but,
when one awakes, it becomes unreal.   (6)

तावत्सत्यं जगद्भाति शुक्तिकारजतं यथा ।
यावन्न ज्ञायते ब्रह्म सर्वाधिष्ठानमव्ययम्   ॥ ७ ॥

Like the (illusion of) silver in mother-
o'-pearl, the world appears to be real only
until the Supreme Self, the immutable
reality behind everything, is realised. (7)

उपादानेऽखिलाधारे जगन्ति परमेश्वरे ।
सर्गस्थितिलयान्यान्ति बुद्बुदानीव वारिणि   ॥ ८ ॥

Like bubbles in water, the worlds are
born, remain and dissolve in the Supreme
Lord that is the material cause and
foundation of all things.   (8)

सच्चिदात्मन्यनुस्यूते नित्ये विष्णौ प्रकल्पिताः ।
व्यक्तयो विविधास्सर्वा हाटके कटकादिवत्   ॥ ९ ॥

On the eternal Vishnu, who is pure
existence and consciousness, as the
common, factor, all these various appear-
ances are super-imposed, like wristlets
and other forms on gold.   (9)

यथाऽऽकाशो हृषीकेशो नानोपाधिगतो विभुः ।
तद्भेदाद्भिन्नवद्भाति तन्नाशे केवलो भवेत्   ॥ १० ॥

Like space, the Lord Vishnu, coming
in contact with various conditions,
appears to be different by reason of their
differences, but is seen to be undifferentiated when those (conditions) are destroyed.   (10)

नानोपाधिवशादेव जातिनामाश्रमादयः ।
आत्मन्यारोपितास्तोये रसवर्णादिभेदवत्   ॥ ११ ॥

Only by virtue of varying conditions
are caste, name, periods of religious life,
etc., imposed on the self, like taste,
colour and other distinctions imposed on
water.   (11)

पञ्चीकृतमहाभूतसम्भवं कर्मसञ्चितम् ।
शरीरं सुखदुःखानां भोगायतनमुच्यते   ॥ १२ ॥

The place for experiencing happiness
and misery, which is made up of the five-
fold compounds of the great elements and
is obtained as the result of past actions,
is called the (dense) body.   (12)

पञ्चप्राणमनोबुद्धिदशेन्द्रियसमन्वितम् ।
अपञ्चीकृतभूतोत्थं सूक्ष्माङ्गं भोगसाधनम्   ॥ १३ ॥

The instrument of enjoyment, which is made up of the uncompounded elements and which consists of the five life-forces, the mind, the consciousness, and the ten senses,* is the subtle body   (13)

अनाद्यविद्याऽनिर्वाच्या कारणोपाधिरुच्यते ।
उपाधित्रितयादन्यमात्मानमवधारयेत्   ॥ १४ ॥

The beginningless illusion that is indefinable is called the casual body. One should understand the self as other than these three bodies (or conditions).   (14)

पञ्चकोशादियोगेन तत्तन्मय इव स्थितः ।
शुद्धात्मा नीलवस्त्रादियोगेन स्फटिको यथा   ॥ १५ ॥

The pure self, by the relation of the five sheaths, etc., appears to assume their respective natures, like a crystal reflecting a blue cloth, etc.   (15)

वपुस्तुषादिभिः कोशैर्युक्तं युक्त्यवघाततः ।
आत्मानमान्तरं शुद्धं विविञ्च्यात्तण्डुलं यथा ॥ १६ ॥

One should separate the grain of the pure inner self from the chaff of the body and other sheaths by the threshing of reason.   (16)

---

*The five senses of preception and the five motor members of the body.

तदा सर्वगतोऽप्यात्मा न सर्वत्रावभासते ।
बुद्धावेवावभासेत स्वच्छेषु प्रतिबिम्बवत् ॥ १७ ॥

Although the self is at all times and in
all things, yet it cannot shine in everything but will shine only in the consciousness, just as a reflection will appear only
in polished surfaces. (17)

देहेन्द्रियमनोबुद्धिप्रकृतिभ्यो विलक्षणम् ।
तद्वृत्तिसाक्षिणं विद्यादात्मानं राजवत्सदा ॥ १८ ॥

One should understand the self to be
always like a king, different from the
body, senses, mind, consciousness, and
eyes, the witness of their activities (18)

व्याप्तेष्विन्द्रियेष्वात्मा व्यापारीवाविवेकिनाम् ।
दृश्यतेऽभ्रेषु धावत्सु धावन्निव यथा शशी ॥ १९ ॥

To the indiscriminating, the self
appears to be active while (in reality) the
senses (alone) are active, in the same way
that the moon is seen as if running, when
the clouds move. (19)

आत्मचैतन्यमाश्रिय देहेन्द्रियमनोधियः ।
स्वक्रियार्थेषु वर्तन्ते सूर्यालोकं यथा जनाः ॥ २० ॥

The body, senses, mind and consciousness, carry on their respective activities
by depending on the consciousness of
the self, like men depending on the sun's
light,   (20)

देहेन्द्रियगुणान्कर्माण्यमले सच्चिदात्मनि ।
अध्यस्यन्त्यविवेकेन गगने नीलतादिवत्   ॥ २१ ॥

Owing to indiscrimination, men attribute the <u>qualities</u> and activities of the
body and the senses to the self that is
pure existence and consciousness*, in the
same way as blue colour is attributed to
the sky.   (21)

अज्ञानान्मानसोपाधेः कर्तृत्वादीनि चात्मनि ।
कल्प्यन्तेऽम्बुगते चन्द्रे चलनादि यथाऽम्भसः ॥२२॥

Moreover, the nature of doer, etc., that
belongs to the conditioning mind is
attributed to the self, just as the motion,
etc., of water is attributed to the reflection
of the moon therein.   (22)

रागेच्छासुखदुःखादि बुद्धौ सत्यां प्रवर्तते ।
सुषुप्तौ नास्ति तन्नाशे तस्माद्बुद्धेस्तु नात्मनः ॥ २३ ॥

Passions, desires, happiness, misery,
etc., exercise their function when the

---

*The self is absolute consciousness as distinguished
from *buddhi*, the individual consciousness.

consciousness is present, and do not exist
in deep sleep when the consciousness is
absent. They belong, therefore, to the
consciousness and not to the self. (23)

प्रकाशोऽर्कस्य तोयस्य शैत्यमग्रेर्यथोष्णता ।
स्वभावस्सच्चिदानन्दनित्यनिर्मलताऽऽत्मनः ॥ २४ ॥

As light is the very nature of the sun,
coldness of water, heat of fire, so are
being consciousness, bliss, eternity and
absoluteness the very nature of the self.

(24)

आत्मनस्सच्चिदंशश्च बुद्धेर्वृत्तिरिति द्वयम् ।
संयोज्य चाविवेकेन जानामीति प्रवर्तते ॥ २५ ॥

By indiscriminately mixing up the
aspect of being and consciousness of the
self with the function of the individual
consciousness, there springs up the idea
" I know." (25)

आत्मनो विक्रिया नास्ति बुद्धेर्बोधो न जात्वपि ।
जीवस्सर्वमलं ज्ञात्वा ज्ञाता द्रष्टेति मुह्यति ॥ २६ ॥

The self undergoes no modification, nor
can knowledge arise in any manner from
individual consciousness (alone). And
yet, one ignorantly imagines that the
individual soul knows, does and sees
everything well. (26)

रज्जुसर्पवदात्मानं जीवं ज्ञात्वा भयं वहेत् ।
नाहं जीवः परात्मेति ज्ञातश्चेन्निर्भयो भवेत् ॥ २७ ॥

By mistaking the self to be the individual soul, as a rope for a serpent, one is
subject to fear. But if he realises, "I am
not the individual soul, but the Supreme
Self," then he is free from fear.   (27)

आत्माऽवभासयत्येको बुद्ध्यादीनीन्द्रियाण्यपि ।
दीपो घटादिवत्स्वात्मा जडैस्तैर्नावभास्यते   ॥ २८ ॥

The self alone illumines the consciousness, the senses, etc., as a light reveals
the pot and other objects; (but) one's
own self is not illumined by these illuminable objects.*   (28)

स्वबोधे नान्यबोधेच्छा बोधरूपतयाऽऽत्मनः ।
न दीपस्यान्यदीपेच्छा यथा स्वात्मप्रकाशने   ॥ २९ ॥

The very nature of the self being knowledge, it does not depend, for a knowledge of itself, on any other knowledge,
in the same way as a light does not need
another light to reveal itself.   (29)

निषिध्य निखिलोपाधीन्नेति नेतीति वाक्यतः ।
विद्यादैक्यं महावाक्यैर्जीवात्मपरमात्मनोः   ॥ ३० ॥

---

*The mind, senses, etc.

Eliminating all limitations with the help of the passage "not this, not this," one should realise the identity of the individual soul and the supreme self by means of the principal scriptural passages. (30)

आविद्यकं शरीरादि दृश्यं बुद्बुदवत्क्षरम् ।

एतद्विलक्षणं विद्यादहं ब्रह्मेति निर्मलम् ॥ ३१ ॥

The body and other objects of perception are the products of ignorance and are as evanescent as bubbles. The self that is unconditioned is other than these and should be understood as "I am Brahman." (31)

देहान्यत्वान्न मे जन्मजराकार्श्यलयादयः ।

शब्दादिविषयैस्सङ्गो निरिन्द्रियतया न च ॥ ३२ ॥

Birth, old age, decay, death, etc., are not for me, because I am other than the body. Sound and other objects of the senses have no connection with me, for I am other than the senses. (32)

अमनस्त्वान्न मे दुःखरागद्वेषभयादयः ।

अप्राणो ह्यमनाः शुभ्र इत्यादिश्रुतिशासनात् ॥ ३३ ॥

I am not the mind, and, therefore, sorrow, desire, hatred, fear, etc., are not for

me. As declared by the scripture, the
self is neither the senses nor mind, but is
unconditioned.   (33)

निर्गुणो निष्क्रियो नित्यो निर्विकल्पो निरञ्जनः ।
निर्विकारो निराकारो नित्यमुक्तोऽस्मि निर्मलः ॥ ३४ ॥

I am attributeless, functionless, eternal,
doubtless, stainless, changeless, formless,
eternally free, and unconditioned.   (34)

अहमाकाशवत्सर्वं बहिरन्तर्गतोऽच्युतः ।
सदा सर्वसमस्सिद्धो निस्सङ्गो निर्मलोऽचलः ॥ ३५ ॥

Like ether, I pervade everything, inside
and outside. I am imperishable, ever the
established (truth), alike to all, unattached, unconditioned, imperturbable.   (35)

नित्यशुद्धविमुक्तैकमखण्डानन्दमद्वयम् ।
सत्यं ज्ञानमनन्तं यत्परं ब्रह्माहमेव तत्   ॥ ३६ ॥

I am that very supreme Brahman that is
reality, knowledge and infinity, that is
ever unconditioned and ever free, the one
undivided bliss that is without a second.
                                                        (36)

एवं निरन्तरकृता ब्रह्मैवास्मीति वासना ।
हर्त्यविद्याविक्षेपान्रोगानिव रसायनम्   ॥ ३७ ॥

Such incessant impression on the mind that "I am only Brahman" removes the turbulences of ignorance, as the elixir of life cures all diseases.   (37)

विविक्तदेश आसीनो विरागो विजितेन्द्रियः ।
भावयेदेकमात्मानं तमनन्तमनन्यधीः   ॥ ३८ ॥

Sitting in a lonely place, free of all passions, with the senses subjugated, one should contemplate that one infinite self, without thinking of anything else.   (38)

आत्मन्येवाखिलं दृश्यं प्रविलाप्य धिया सुधीः ।
भावयेदेकमात्मानं निर्मलाकाशवत्सदा   ॥ ३९ ॥

A wise man should, by his intelligence, submerge, in the self all that is objective and should ever contemplate the one self that is like unlimited space.   (39)

रूपवर्णादिकं सर्वं विहाय परमार्थवित् ।
परिपूर्णचिदानन्दस्वरूपेणावतिष्ठते   ॥ ४० ॥

One who has realised the supreme truth gives up everything, such as form, caste, etc., and abides, by nature, in (the self, that is,) infinite consciousness and bliss.   (40)

ज्ञातृज्ञानज्ञेयभेदः परे नात्मनि विद्यते ।
चिदानन्दैकरूपत्वाद्दीप्यते स्वयमेव तत् ॥ ४१ ॥

The distinction of knower, knowledge
and the known does not exist in respect
of the supreme self. Being sole consciousness and bliss, it shines by itself
alone. (41)

एवमात्मारणौ ध्यानमथने सततं कृते ।
उदिताऽवगतिज्वाला सर्वाज्ञानेन्धनं दहेत् ॥ ४२ ॥

The flame of knowledge that arises by
this constant churning of meditation on
the wood* of the self, will completely
burn away the fuel of ignorance. (42)

अरुणेनेव बोधेन पूर्वं सन्तमसे हृते ।
तत आविर्भवेदात्मा स्वयमेवांशुमानिव ॥ ४३ ॥

When knowledge has destroyed ignorance, the self will manifest itself, in the
same way as the sun rises as soon as the
dawn † of day has dispelled darkness.
(43)

आत्मा तु सततं प्राप्तोऽप्यप्राप्तवदविद्यया ।
तन्नाशे प्राप्तवद्भाति स्वकण्ठाभरणं यथा ॥ ४४ ॥

---

*Arani wood, use to kindle fire for sacrifices by
churning it.

† Aruna, the charioteer of the sun; the dawn-god.

The self, that is ever with us, appears,
by ignorance. as if it were unattained
and, when that (ignorance) is destroyed,
attained, like one's own necklace. *   (44)

स्थाणौ पुरुषवद्भ्रान्त्या कृता ब्रह्मणि जीवता ।
जीवस्य तात्त्विके रूपे तस्मिन्दृष्टे निवर्तते   ॥ ४५ ॥

The condition of individual soul has
been imposed on Brahman by illusion, as
the form of a man on a post, but disappears when the true nature of the individual soul is realised.   (45)

तत्त्वस्वरूपानुभवादुत्पन्नं ज्ञानमञ्जसा ।
अहं ममेति चाज्ञानं बाधते दिग्भ्रमादिवत्   ॥ ४६ ॥

The knowledge that arises from the
realisation of one's own true nature.
directly destroys the illusion of "I" and
"mine" which resembles the confusion of
the directions.†   (46)

सम्यग्विज्ञानवान्योगी स्वात्मन्येवाखिलं स्थितम् ।
एकं च सर्वमात्मानमीक्षते ज्ञानचक्षुषा   ॥ ४७ ॥

---

*One appears to search for his necklace and find
it, although it has been on his neck all the time.

† One who mistakes the directions, north, east, etc.,
corrects himself as soon as he clearly understands his
own position.

The devotee (*yogin*) that has gained right realisation sees all things, by the eye of knowledge, as existing in his own self, and the one self as all things.   (47)

आत्मैवेदं जगत्सर्वमात्मनोऽन्यन्न किञ्चन ।
मृदो यद्वद्घटादीनि स्वात्मानं सर्वमीक्षते   ॥ ४८ ॥

He sees all things as his own self in the same way as one sees pots, etc,, as (mere) clay ; (for), all this universe is only the self, and there is naught other than the self.   (48)

जीवन्मुक्तिस्तु तद्विद्वान्पूर्वोपाधिगुणांस्त्यजेत् ।
स सच्चिदादिधर्मत्वाद्भेजे भ्रमरकीटवत्   ॥ ४९ ॥

Liberation-while-living means that the wise person, having abandoned his former limitations and qualities, and acquiring the properties of being, consciousness (and bliss), attains Brahman, in the same way as the worm becomes the wasp.   (49)

तीर्त्वा मोहार्णवं हत्वा रागद्वेषादिराक्षसान् ।
योगी शान्तिसमायुक्त आत्मारामो विराजते   ॥ ५० ॥

Having crossed the ocean of ignorance and having slain the demons of likes and

dislikes, etc., the seer, united to tranquillity, is supremely happy in the enjoyment of the bliss of his own self.*   (50)

बाह्यानित्यसुखासक्तिं हित्वाऽऽत्मसुखनिर्वृतः ।
घटस्थदीपवच्छश्वदन्तरेव प्रकाशते   ॥ ५१ ॥

Leaving aside all attachments to external and transient pleasures, and happy
in the bliss of the self, such a one, for
ever, shines within, like a light inside a
globe.   (51)

उपाधिस्थोऽपि तद्धर्मैरलिप्तो व्योमवन्मुनिः ।
सर्वविन्मूढवत्तिष्ठेदसक्तो वायुवच्चरेत्   ॥ ५२ ॥

The seer, though remaining amidst
limitations, should yet be unaffected by
their qualities, like space. Knowing all,
he should be like one that knows not, and
should wander about, unattached, like
the wind.   (52)

उपाधिविलयाद्विष्णौ निर्विशेषं विशेन्मुनिः ।
जले जलं वियद्व्योम्नि तेजस्तेजसि वा यथा ॥ ५३ ॥

When the limitations disappear, the
seer merges unreservedly in the Supreme

*This is an allegorical explanation, incidentally of
the story of the Ramayana.

(*vishnu*), like water in water, space in
space, or light in light. (53)

यल्लाभान्नापरो लाभो यत्सुखान्नापरं सुखम् ।
यज्ज्ञानान्नापरं ज्ञानं तद्ब्रह्मेत्यवधारयेत् ॥ ५४ ॥

Than gaining which there is no greater
gain, than whose bliss there is no higher
bliss, than knowing which there is no
higher knowledge,—that should be
understood as Brahman. (54)

यद्दृष्ट्वा नापरं दृश्यं यद्भूत्वा नापुनर्भवः ।
यज्ज्ञात्वा नापरं ज्ञेयं तद्ब्रह्मेत्यवधारयेत् ॥ ५५ ॥

Seeing which naught else remains to
be seen, becoming which there is no becoming* again, knowing which naught
else remains to be known,—that should
be understood as Brahman. (55)

तिर्यगूर्ध्वमधः पूर्णं सच्चिदानन्दमद्वयम् ।
अनन्तं नित्यमेकं यत्तद्ब्रह्मेत्यवधारयेत् ॥ ५६ ॥

That which is all-pervading, around,
above, below, which is being, consciousness and bliss, which is without a second,

---

*Birth.

without end, eternal, sole,—that should
be understood as Brahman.   (56)

अतद्व्यावृत्तिरूपेण वेदान्तैर्लक्ष्यतेऽन्ययम् ।
अखण्डानन्दमेकं यत्तद्ब्रह्मेत्यवधारयेत्   ॥ ५७ ॥

The immutable, the one uninterrupted
bliss, which is indicated by the Vedanta
by excluding what is not it,—that should
be understood as Brahman.   (57)

अखण्डानन्दरूपस्य तस्यानन्दलवाश्रिताः ।
ब्रह्माद्यास्तारतम्येन भवन्त्यानन्दिनो लवाः   ॥ ५८ ॥

(The four-faced) Brahma and others,
that are but parts of that self which is
uninterrupted bliss, become happy, each
in his own degree, by possessing a parti-
cle of that bliss.   (58)

तद्युक्तमखिलं वस्तु व्यवहारश्चिदन्वितः ।
तस्मात्सर्वगतं ब्रह्म क्षीरे सर्पिरिवाखिले   ॥ ५९ ॥

Every object (is such because it) pos-
sesses that. All activity has consciousness running through it.*   The Supreme

---

*These are the *sat* (being) and *chit* (consciousness)
aspects of the self. The *ananda* (bliss) aspect has
been dealt with in the previous verse.

Self, therefore, pervades the whole universe, as butter is in every part of milk.

(59)

अनण्वस्थूलमह्रस्वमदीर्घमजमव्ययम् ।
अरूपगुणवर्णाख्यं तद्ब्रह्मेत्यवधारयेत्   ॥ ६० ॥

That which is neither subtle nor dense,
neither short nor long, which is unborn,
immutable, devoid of form, quality, caste
or name,—that should be understood as
Brahman.   (60)

यद्भासा भासतेऽर्कादि भास्यैर्यत्तु न भास्यते ।
येन सर्वमिदं भाति तद्ब्रह्मेत्यवधारयेत्   ॥ ६१ ॥

By whose light the sun, etc., shine, but
which is not illumined by these that are
illuminable, and by virtue of which all
this (universe) shines*,—that should be
understood as Brahman.   (61)

स्वयमन्तर्बहिर्व्याप्य भासयन्नखिलं जगत् ।
ब्रह्म प्रकाशते वह्निप्रतप्तायसपिण्डवत्   ॥ ६२ ॥

Pervading the whole universe, internally and externally, and illumintng it,
the Brahman shines by itself, like a red-
hot iron ball.   (62)

---

*Is manifest; is perceived.

जगद्विलक्षणं ब्रह्म ब्रह्मणोऽन्यन्न किञ्चन ।

ब्रह्मान्यद्भाति चेन्मिथ्या यथा मरुमरीचिका ॥ ६३ ॥

The Brahman is different from the universe. There is naught other than
Brahman. If anything other than Brahman is perceived, it is as unreal as the
mirage in the desert.   (63)

दृश्यते श्रूयते यद्यद्ब्रह्मणोऽन्यन्न तद्भवेत् ।

तत्त्वज्ञानाच्च तद्ब्रह्म सच्चिदानन्दमद्वयम् ॥ ६४ ॥

Whatever is seen or heard, other than
Brahman, cannot be (real). Even that is
Brahman, the secondless being, consciousness and bliss, when the reality is
known.   (64)

सर्वगं सच्चिदानन्दं ज्ञानचक्षुर्निरीक्षते ।

अज्ञानचक्षुर्नेक्षेत भास्वन्तं भानुमन्धवत् ॥ ६५ ॥

He who has the eye of knowledge sees
Brahman that is being, consciousness and
bliss, in all things; but he who has not
the eye of knowledge cannot see it thus,
as a blind man cannot see the shining
sun.   (65)

श्रवणादिभिरुद्दीप्तज्ञानाग्निपरितापितः ।

जीवस्सर्वदलान्मुक्तः स्वर्णवद् द्योतते स्वयम् ॥ ६६ ॥

The individual soul, melted in the fire
of knowledge kindled by instruction,

etc., is free from all taints, like gold, and
shines by itself. (66)

हृदाकाशोदितो ह्यात्मा बोधभानुस्तमोऽपहृत् ।
सर्वव्यापी सर्वधारी भाति भासयतेऽखिलम् ॥ ६७ ॥

The self is the sun of knowledge that,
rising in the firmament of the heart, destroys the darkness of ignorance, and,
pervading all and supporting all, shines
and makes everything shine. (67)

दिग्देशकालाद्यनपेक्ष्य सर्वगं
    शीतादिहृन्नित्यसुखं निरञ्जनम् ।
यस्स्वात्मतीर्थं भजते विनिष्क्रियः
    स सर्ववित्सर्वगतोऽमृतो भवेत् ॥ ६८ ॥

He who, unmindful of (the limitations
of) direction, space, time, etc., and perfectly tranquil, attains the sanctum of the
self, that is the all-pervading, stainless,
eternal bliss which dispels (all qualities
like heart and cold), etc.,—he becomes
all-knowing, all-pervading, and immortal.
(68)

॥ इत्यात्मबोधः समाप्तः ॥
Thus ends Knowledge of Self.

॥ वाक्यवृत्ति: ॥

COMMENTARY ON THE TEXT

सर्गस्थितिप्रलयहेतुमचिन्त्यशक्तिं
विश्वेश्वरं विदितविश्वमनन्तमूर्तिम् ।
निर्मुक्तबन्धनमपारसुखाम्बुराशिं
श्रीवल्लभं विमलबोधघनं नमामि ॥ १ ॥

I salute the Lord of Lakshmi, the cause of creation, preservation and dissolution, the Lord of the universe possessing in conceivable power, omniscient, infinite in form, free of all bondage, the ocean of unbounded bliss, the concentration of pure knowledge. (1)

यस्य प्रसादादहमेव विष्णुः
मय्येव सर्वं परिकल्पितं च ।
इत्थं विजानामि सदाऽत्मरूपं
तस्यांघ्रिपद्मं प्रणतोऽस्मि नित्यम् ॥ २ ॥

I ever prostrate to the lotus-feet of Him by whose grace I always realise the nature of the self to the effect that I alone am the Supreme and that all things are merely superimposed on me. (2)

तापत्रयार्केसन्तप्तः कश्चिदुद्विग्नमानसः ।
शमादिसाधनैर्युक्तः सद्गुरुं परिपृच्छति   ॥ ३ ॥

Sorely afflicted by the sun of the three
miseries*, and perplexed in mind, some
one, after acquiring the qualifications of
mind-control, etc., asks the good Master
as follows :   (3)

अनायासेन येनास्मान्मुच्येयं भवबन्धनात् ।
तन्मे संक्षिप्य भगवन्केवलं कृपया वद   ॥ ४ ॥

O Lord, out of mere mercy, tell me
briefly how I may, without (much) effort,
be liberated from this bondage of births
and deaths.   (4)

साध्वी ते वचनव्यक्तिः प्रतिभाति वदामि ते ।
इदं तदिति विस्पष्टं सावधानमतिः शृणु   ॥ ५ ॥

(The Master replies :) The manner of
thy speech seems to me to be excellent.
I shall explain to thee clearly which is
which.   Listen with an attentive mind.
                                                (5)

---

*See footnote on page 86.

तत्त्वमस्यादिवाक्योत्थं यज्जीवपरमात्मनोः ।
तादात्म्यविषयं ज्ञानं तदिदं मुक्तिसाधनम् ॥ ६ ॥

The knowledge relating to the identity
of the individual soul and the Supreme
Self that arises from texts like "That
thou art," is the means to liberation. (6)

को जीवः कः परश्चात्मा तादात्म्यं वा कथं तयोः ।
तत्त्वमस्यादिवाक्यं वा कथं तत्प्रतिपादयेत् ॥ ७ ॥

What is the individual soul? What is
the Supreme Self? How can there be
identity between the two? And how can
texts like "That thou art" express the
same? (7)

अत्र ब्रूमः समाधानं कोऽन्यो जीवस्त्वमेव हि ।
यस्त्वं पृच्छसि मां कोऽहं ब्रह्मैवासि न संशयः ॥ ८

We shall explain it (thus). What else,
indeed, is the individual soul except
thou alone. Thou that questionest me,
'who am I', art Brahman itself, without
doubt. (8)

पदार्थमेव जानामि नाद्यापि भगवन् स्फुटम् ।
अहं ब्रह्मेति वाक्यार्थं प्रतिपद्ये कथं वद ॥ ९ ॥

I have not yet clearly grasped, O Lord,
even the meaning of the words, "I am
Brahman." How can I understand, tell
me the meaning of the sentence (as a
whole)?   (9)

सत्यमाह भवानत्र विगानं नैव विद्यते ।
हेतु: पदार्थबोधो हि वाक्यार्थावगतेरिह   ॥ १० ॥

What thou sayest is true and free from
reproach. For, a knowledge of the word-
meaning is indeed essential for the understanding of the sentence-meaning. (10)

अन्त:करणतद्वृत्तिसाक्षिचैतन्यविग्रह: ।
आनन्दरूप: सत्य: सन्कि नात्मानं प्रपद्यते   ॥ ११ ॥

Why dost thou not understand thyself,
—thou whose very nature is reality and
bliss and (pure) consciousness that is the
witness of the individual consciousness
and all its workings?   (11)

सत्यानन्दस्वरूपं धीसाक्षिणं ज्ञानविग्रहम् ।
चिन्तयात्मतया नित्यं त्यक्त्वा देहादिगां धियम् ॥

Leaving aside all thought relating to
the body, etc., thou shouldst ever medi-

tate upon that whose nature is reality,
bliss, and knowledge and which is the
witness of consciousness, as thyself.   (12)

रूपादिमान्यतः पिण्डस्ततो नात्मा घटादिवत् ।
वियदादिमहाभूतविकारत्वाच्च कुम्भवत्   ॥ १३ ॥

Because the body has form, etc., like
an earthen vessel or other object, and is,
like an earthen vessel, composed of the
(five) great elements, ether, etc., it cannot
be the self.   (13)

अनात्मा यदि पिण्डोऽयमुक्तहेतुबलान्मतः ।
करामलकवत्साक्षादात्मानं प्रतिपादय   ॥ १४ ॥

If, for the reasons aforesaid. this body
is not the self, reveal the self, then, as
clearly as a berry in the hand.   (14)

घटद्रष्टा घटाद्भिन्नः सर्वथा न घटो यथा ।
देहद्रष्टा तथा देहो नाहमित्यवधारय   ॥ १५ ॥

As the witness of an earthen pot is
different from the pot and is not the pot
in any sense, so is the witness ef the
body. Understand, therefore, "I am not
the body."   (15)

एवमिन्द्रियट्ठ्नाहमिन्द्रियाणीति निश्चिनु ।
मनो बुद्धिस्तथा प्राणो नाहमित्यवधारय   ॥ १६ ॥

Conclude, in the same way, "I am the witness of the senses and not the senses themselves." So, too, understand, "I am not the mind, the consciousness, or the life-force." (16)

संघातोऽपि तथा नाहमिति दृश्यविलक्षणम् ।
द्रष्टारमनुमानेन निपुणं संप्रधारय   ॥ १७ ॥

Also "I am not the combination (of these)." Understand, thus, by intelligent reasoning, the witness that is distinct from the object. (17)

देहेन्द्रियादयो भावा हानादिन्याप्तृतिक्षमाः ।
यस्य सन्निधिमात्रेण सोऽहमित्यवधारय   ॥ १८ ॥

Understand "I am He by whose mere proximity, the body, senses and other objects become capable of (all) activities like selection, etc. (18)

अनापन्नविकारः सन्त्रयस्कान्तवदेव यः ।
बुद्ध्यादीश्चालयेत्प्रत्यक् सोऽहमित्यवधारय   ॥ १९ ॥

Understand 'I am that inner self which impels the consciousness, etc., but is itself unchanging, like the lodestone.

(19)

अजडात्मवदाभान्ति यत्सान्निध्याज्जडा अपि ।
देहेन्द्रियमनःप्राणाः सोऽहमित्यवधारय ॥ २० ॥

Understand "I am He by whose, proximity, the body, senses, mind, and life-forces, though motionless, yet seem like the self that is not so. (20)

अगमन्मे मनोऽन्यत्र साम्प्रतं च स्थिरीकृतम् ।
एवं यो वेद धीवृत्तिं सोऽहमित्यवधारय ॥ २१ ॥

"My mind had gone elsewhere, but has now been steadied." Understand "I am He who knows the above activity of the mind." (21)

स्वप्रजागरिते सुप्तिं भावाभावौ धियां तथा ।
यो वेत्त्यविक्रियः साक्षात्सोऽहमित्यवधारय ॥ २२ ॥

Understand "I am He who is the direct witness, himself changeless, of waking, dream and sleep, and of the presence and absence of objects, and of all phases of consciousness. (22)

घटावभासको दीपो घटादन्यो यथेष्यते ।
देहावभासको देही तथाऽहं बोधविग्रहः ॥ २३ ॥

As it is admitted that the light revealing (the presence of) a pot is other than
the pot, so am I of the nature of knowledge, the dweller in the body that
reveals the body. (23)

पुत्रवित्तादयो भावा यस्य शेषतया प्रियाः ।
द्रष्टा सर्वप्रियतमः सोऽहमित्यवधारय ॥ २४ ॥

Understand "I am the witness that is
the dearest of all, for whose sake alone,
sons, wealth and other objects are dear."
(24)

परप्रेमास्पदतया मा न भूवमहं सदा ।
भूयासमिति यो द्रष्टा सोऽहमित्यवधारय ॥ २५ ॥

Understand "I am the witness who, being himself the object of highest love,
feels 'let me never cease to be, but let me
ever exist'." (25)

यः साक्षिलक्षणो बोधस्त्वंपदार्थः स उच्यते ।
साक्षित्वमपि बुद्धत्वमविकारितयाऽऽत्मनः ॥ २६ ॥

The consciousness that is the witness
is said to be the meaning of the word

"thou." The self is the witness and the knower, because it is devoid of change. (26)

देहेन्द्रियमनःप्राणाहंकृतिभ्यो विलक्षणः ।
प्रोज्झिताशेषषड्भावविकारस्त्वंपदाभिधः ॥ २७ ॥

By the word "thou" is denoted that which is different from the body, senses, mind, life-forces, and ego, and is entirely devoid of the six states* or other change. (27)

त्वमर्थमेवं निश्चित्य तदर्थं चिन्तयेत्पुनः ।
अतद्व्यावृत्तिरूपेण साक्षाद्विधिमुखेन च ॥ २८ ॥

Having thus understood the meaning of "thou," one should then contemplate the meaning of "that," both by eliminating what is not 'that' and by means of direct definitions thereof. (28)

निरस्ताशेषसंसारदोषोऽस्थूलादिलक्षणः ।
अदृश्यत्वादिगुणकः पराक्ततमोमलः ॥ २९ ॥

Bereft of taint of phenomenal existence, characterised by phrases like "not dense, etc." qualified by non-objectivity, etc,, free from the stain of nescience. (29)

---

*Birth, existence, growth, maturity, decay, and death.

निरस्तातिशयानन्दः सत्यप्रज्ञानविग्रहः ।
सत्तास्वलक्षणः पूर्णः परमात्मेति गीयते   ॥ ३० ॥

Bliss unsurpassed, reality, knowledge,
and existence by nature, all-filling,—
'that' is spoken of as the Supreme Self.

(30)

सर्वज्ञत्वं परेशत्वं तथा सम्पूर्णशक्तिता ।
वेदैः समर्थ्यते यस्य तद्ब्रह्मेत्यवधारय   ॥ ३१ ॥

Understand that to be the Brahman in
respect of which the Vedas assert omniscience, supreme lordship and omnipo-
tence.   (31)

यज्ज्ञानात्सर्वविज्ञानं श्रुतिषु प्रतिपादितम् ।
मृदाद्यनेकदृष्टान्तैस्तद्ब्रह्मेत्यवधारय   ॥ ३२ ॥

Understand that to be the Brahman of
which the Vedas explain, by various
illustrations like clay*, etc., that, by
knowing it all things are known.   (32)

यदानन्त्यं प्रतिज्ञाय श्रुतिस्तत्सिद्धये जगौ ।
तत्कार्यत्वं प्रपञ्चस्य तद्ब्रह्मेत्यवधारय   ॥ ३३ ॥

---

*By knowing clay, all clay things like pot, etc., are
known.

Understand that to be the Brahman, of which, the Vedas enunciate infinitude and, to establish it, declare the universe to be the effect of that.* (33)

विजिज्ञास्यतया यच्च वेदान्तेषु मुमुक्षुभिः ।
समर्थ्यतेऽतियत्नेन तद्ब्रह्मेत्यवधारय ॥ ३४ ॥

Understand that to be the Brahman which in the Vedanta, is established, by close reasoning, as the (only) thing to be realised by the aspirants for liberation.

(34)

जीवात्मना प्रवेशश्च नियन्तृत्वं च तान्प्रति ।
श्रूयते यस्य वेदेषु तद्ब्रह्मेत्यवधारय ॥ ३५ ॥

Understand that to be the Brahman which is spoken of in the Vedas as having entered all beings as their souls and controlling them. (35)

कर्मणां फलदातृत्वं यस्यैव श्रूयते श्रुतौ ।
जीवानां हेतुकर्तृत्वं तद्ब्रह्मेत्यवधारय ॥ ३६ ॥

Understand that to be the Brahman which alone is spoken of in the Vedas as the bestower of the reward of actions and the originator of the cause † of individual existence. (36)

---

*i.e., Brahman is the cause of the universe.
† Maya or nescience.

तत्त्वंपदार्थौ निर्णीतौ वाक्यार्थश्चिन्त्यतेऽधुना ।
तादात्म्यमत्र वाक्यार्थस्तयोरेव पदार्थयोः   ॥ ३७ ॥

The meanings of the words 'that' and
'thou' have been determined. The meaning of the sentence will now be dealt
with. This sentence-meaning is the
identity between those same two word-
meanings.   (37)

संसर्गो वा विशिष्टो वा वाक्यार्थो नात्र सम्मतः ।
अखण्डैकरसत्वेन वाक्यार्थो विदुषां मतः   ॥ ३८ ॥

The accepted meaning of the sentence,
in this case, is neither co-existence nor
particularisation, The meaning of the
sentence, as accepted by the wise, is
essential identity without reservation.

(38)

प्रत्यग्बोधो य आभाति सोऽद्वयानन्दलक्षणः ।
अद्वयानन्दरूपश्च प्रत्यग्बोधैकलक्षणः   ॥ ३९ ॥

What appears as the inner consciousness is that whose characteristic is
secondless bliss, whose nature is secondless bliss, and whose sole definition is
inner consciousness.   (39)

इत्थमन्योन्यतादात्म्यप्रतिपत्तिर्यदा भवेत् ।
अब्रह्मत्वं त्वमर्थस्य व्यावर्तेत तदैव हि   ॥ ४० ॥

When the mutual identity of the two is
thus understood, then only will the non-
Brahmanness of the word-meaning 'thou'
be eliminated, (40)

तदर्थस्य च पारोक्ष्यं यद्येवं किं ततः शृणु ।
पूर्णानन्दैकरूपेण प्रत्यग्बोधोऽवतिष्ठते ॥ ४१ ॥

as also the unknownness of the word-
meaning of 'that.' If it be so, what then ?
Listen. The inner consciousness remains
absolutely as infinite bliss by nature. (41)

तत्त्वमस्यादिवाक्यं च तादात्म्यप्रतिपादने ।
लक्ष्यौ तत्त्वपदार्थौ द्वावुपादाय प्रवर्तते ॥ ४२ ॥

Further, a sentence like 'that thou art,'
in order to denote identity, proceeds on
the basis of the secondary* meaning of
the two words 'that' and 'thou.' (42)

हित्वा द्वौ शबलौ वाच्यौ वाक्यं वाक्यार्थबोधने ।
यथा प्रवर्ततेऽस्माभिस्तथा व्याख्यातमादरात् ॥ ४३ ॥

We shall carefully explain how the
sentence makes its own meaning clear by
excluding the expressed meaning of the
two words, which are mixed up. (43)

---

*Lakshya, secondary, indirect or derived, as oppos-
ed to vachya, primary, direct or expressed.

आलम्बनतया भाति योऽसत्प्रत्ययशब्दयोः ।
अन्तःकरणसंभिन्नबोधः स त्वंपदाभिधः   ॥ ४४ ॥

The consciousness, conditioned by the mind, which appears as the connecting link between the idea "I" and the word "I", is expressed by the word "thou".

(44)

मायोपाधिर्जगद्योनिः सर्वज्ञत्वादिलक्षणः ।
पारोक्ष्यशबलः सत्याद्यात्मकस्तत्पदाभिधः   ॥ ४५ ॥

The first cause of the worlds, conditioned by nescience (*maya*), characterised by omniscience, etc.*, of the nature of reality†, etc.†, and affected by non-cognisability, is expressed by the word "that".

(45)

प्रत्यक्परोक्षतैकस्य स द्वितीयत्वपूर्णता ।
विरुध्यते यतस्तस्माल्लक्षणा सम्प्रवर्तते   ॥ ४६ ॥

(But) cognisability and non-cognisability, having a second and being infinite, are inconsistent in respect of the same thing. Hence is the necessity for the derived (or secondary) meaning. (46)

मानान्तरविरोधे तु मुख्यार्थस्य परिग्रहे ।
मुख्यार्थेनाविनाभूते प्रतीतिर्लक्षणोच्यते   ॥ ४७ ॥

---

*Omniscience, omnipotence, omnipresence.
† Reality, knowledge, infinity.

When the adoption of the primary meaning is inconsistent with other (established) proofs, the adoption of **a** meaning not unconnected with the principal meaning, is called the derivation of meaning (*lakshana*).   (47)

तत्त्वमस्यादिवाक्येषु लक्षणा भागलक्षणा ।

सोऽयमित्यादिवाक्यस्थपदयोरिव नापरा   ॥ ४८ ॥

The derivation of meaning, in the case of passages like "that thou art", is a partial derivation, and no other, as in the case of the words in sentences like "This is he".   (48)

अहं ब्रह्मेति वाक्यार्थबोधो यावद्दृढीभवेत् ।

शमादिसहितस्तावदभ्यसेच्छ्रवणादिकम्   ॥ ४९ ॥

Until the sentence-meaning of "I am Brahman') is firmly understood, so long should one possess control of mind, etc., and practise (the expedients of hearing,* etc.).   (49)

श्रुत्याचार्यप्रसादेन दृढबोधो यदा भवेत् ।

निरस्ताशेषसंसारनिदानः पुरुषस्तदा   ॥ ५० ॥

When, by the grace of the Vedic teacher, one gets a firm understanding (of the above sentence), then is he entirely free from phenomenal condition and its cause.†   (50)

---

*Hearing, meditation and concentration.

† Nescience or *maya*.

विशीर्णकार्यंकरणो भूतसूक्ष्मैरनावृतः ।

विमुक्तकर्मनिगलः सद्य एव विमुच्यते   ॥ ५१ ॥

All ends and means destroyed, unconditioned by the elements and the subtler
bodies, and free from the bonds of action,
such a one is immediately liberated. (51)

प्रारब्धकर्मवेगेन जीवन्मुक्तो यदा भवेत् ।

किञ्चित्कालमनारब्धकर्मबन्धस्य संक्षये   ॥ ५२ ॥

When by the destruction of the bondage of past actions not yet ripe for enjoyment, one becomes liberated while
living, he remains as such for a short
time by virtue of such of his past actions
as have brought about his present life.

(52)

निरस्तातिशयानन्दं वैष्णवं परमं पदम् ।

पुनरावृत्तिरहितं कैवल्यं प्रतिपद्यते   ॥ ५३ ॥

(Thereafter) he attains absolute liberation without any more birth, which is of
the nature of unsurpassed bliss and is
known as the supreme abode of Vishnu.

(53)

॥ इति वाक्यवृत्तिः सम्पूर्णा ॥

Here ends the Commentary on the Text.

DEFINITION OF ONE'S OWN SELF

॥ स्वात्मनिरूपणम् ॥

श्रीगुरुचरणद्वन्द्वं वन्देऽहं मथितदुःसहद्वन्द्वम् ।
भ्रान्तिग्रहोपशान्ति पांसुमयं यस्य भसितमातनुते ॥१॥

I salute the two feet of the holy Master,
which destroy (this) unendurable duality,
and whose dust, like the sacred ashes,
quell the demon of illusion.   (1)

देशिकवरं दयालुं वन्देऽहं निहतसकलसन्देहम् ।
यच्चरणद्वयमद्वयमनुभवमुपदिशति तत्पदस्यार्थम् ॥२॥

I salute the merciful and most excellent
Master who destroys all doubts and whose
two feet reveal the enjoyment of one-ness
as the meaning of the word "that".   (2)

संसारदावपावकसन्तप्तः सकलसाधनोपेतः ।
स्वात्मनिरूपणनिपुणैः वाक्यैः शिष्यः प्रबोध्यते गुरुणा ॥

Scorched by the forest-fire of phenomenal existence, the pupil, possessed of
all necessary qualifications, is thus enlightened by the Master with words
capable of revealing the true self.   (3)

अस्ति स्वयमित्यस्मिन् अर्थे कस्यास्ति संशयः पुंसः ।
अत्रापि संशयश्चेत् संशयिता यस्स एव भवसि त्वम् ॥

Whoever doubts the fact that himself
exists? If even this is doubted, he who
doubts is only thyself. (4)

नाहमिति वेत्ति योऽसौ सत्यं ब्रह्मैव वेत्ति नास्तीति ।
अहमस्मीति विजानन् ब्रह्मैवासौ स्वयं विजानाति ॥

When one knows "I am not", it is
verily Brahman itself that knows "it is
not." When one knows "I am", then (too)
it is that Brahman itself that knows
thus. (5)

ब्रह्म त्वमेव तस्मात् नाहं ब्रह्मेति मोहमात्रमिदम् ।
मोहेन भवति भेदः क्लेशाः सर्वे भवन्ति तन्मूलाः ॥६॥

Thyself, therefore, art Brahman. "I am
not Brahman" is a mere illusion. From
illusion springs separation* wherein all
sorrows have root. (6)

न क्लेशपञ्चकमिदं भजते कृतकोशपञ्चकविवेकः ।
अत एव पञ्च कोशान् कुशलधियः सन्ततं विचिन्वन्ति ॥

---

* Difference, duality, manifoldness, variety.

He who gains a clear knowledge of the
five sheaths (of the self) does not experience the five sufferings,* The wise, therefore, always investigate the five sheaths.
(7)

अन्नप्राणमनोमयविज्ञानानन्दपञ्चकोशानाम् ।
एकैकान्तर्भाजां भजति विवेकात्प्रकाश्यतामात्मा ॥८॥

By a clear knowledge of the five
sheaths, *anna-maya*, *prana-maya*, *mano-
maya*, *vijnana-maya* and *ananda-maya*, each
within the one before it, the self becomes
capable of being revealed.   (8)

वपुरिदमन्नमयाख्यः कोशो नात्मा जडो घटप्रायः ।
प्रागुत्पत्तेः पश्चात् तदभावस्यापि दृश्यमानत्वात् ॥९॥

This (gross) body which is called the
anna-maya sheath, is not the self, for it is
non-sentient, almost like an earthen vessel. and is non-existent before birth and
after death.   (9)

कोशः प्राणमयोऽयं वायुविशेषो वपुष्यवच्छिन्नः ।
अस्य कथमात्मता स्यात् क्षुत्तृष्णाभ्यामुपेयुषः पीडाम् ॥

---

* *Avidya*, ignorance ; *asmita*, egoism ; *ruga*, desire ;
Avesha hate, and *abhinivesa*, fear of death.

So much of the atmosphere as is contained by the body is the *prana-maya* sheath. How can this be the self, being afflicted with hunger and thirst? (10)

कुरुते वपुष्यहन्तां गेहादौ यः करोति ममतां च ।
रागद्वेषविधेयो नासावात्मा मनोमयः कोशः ॥ ११ ॥

Nor can be *mano-maya* sheath be the self, which thinks of the body as 'I' and of home, etc., as 'mine', and which is the slave of likes and dislikes. (11)

सुप्तौ स्वयं विलीना बोधे व्याप्ता कलेवरं सकलम् ।
विज्ञानशब्दवाच्या चित्प्रतिबिम्बा न बुद्धिरप्यात्मा ॥

Nor can the individual consciousness known by the name of *vijnana-maya* (sheath) be the self, for it is only a reflection of the pure consciousness,* disappearing in deep sleep and permeating the whole body in conscious moments.

(12)

सुप्तिगतैः सुखलेशैः अभिमनुते यः सुखी भवामीति ।
आनन्दकोशनामा सोऽहङ्कारः कथं भवेदात्मा ॥ १३ ॥

---
* The Supreme Self.

How can I-ness (or egoism), which is called the *ananda-maya* sheath, be the self, fondly imagining "I am happy" by reason of the small fractions of bliss found in deep sleep? (13)

यः स्फुरति बिम्बभूतः स भवेदानन्द एव सकलात्मा ।
प्रागूर्ध्वेमपि च सत्त्वात् अविकारित्वादबाध्यमानत्वात्।।

That which shines as the reality is bliss itself, is the self of all, for it exists before and after, is changeless and un-contradictable. (14)

अन्नमयादेरस्मात् अपरं यदि नानुभूयते किञ्चित् ।
अनुभविताऽन्नमयादेः अस्तीत्यस्मिन्न कश्चिदपलापः ॥

If nothing different from the *annamaya* and other sheaths is perceived, it cannot nevertheless be denied that there is one that perceives the *annamaya*, etc., sheaths. (15)

स्वयमेवानुभवत्वात् यद्यप्येतस्य नानुभाव्यत्वम् ।
सकृदप्यभावशङ्का न भवेद्बोधस्वरूपसत्तायाः ॥ १६ ॥

Although the self, being of the very nature of consciousness, cannot therefore be the object of consciousness, nevertheless there can never be a doubt regarding the absolute existence of consciousness itself. (16)

अनुभवति विश्वमात्मा विश्वेनासौ न चानुभूयेत ।
न खलु प्रकाश्यतेऽसौ विश्वमशेषं प्रकाशयन्भानुः ॥

The self experiences all things, but
cannot be experienced by anything. The
sun, that illumines the whole world, is
not, in its turn, illumined. (17)

तदिदं ताद्टशमीद्टशमेतावत्तावदिति च यन्न भवेत् ।
ब्रह्म तदित्यवधेयं नो चेद्विषयो भवेत्परोक्षं च ॥ १८ ॥

What is neither that nor this, so or
thus, that much or this, much,—that
should be understood to be Brahman.
Otherwise, it will be a mere object, and
not directly knowable. (18)

इदमिदमिति प्रतीते वस्तुनि सर्वत्र बाध्यमानेऽपि ।
अनिदमबाध्यं तत्त्वं सत्त्वादेतस्य न च परोक्षत्वम् ॥

While everything that is perceived as
'this, this' is contradictable*, the reality
that is 'not this' is not contradictable. It
is, moreover, not unrealisable, because it
exists. (19)

नावेद्यमपि परोक्षं भवति ब्रह्म स्वयंप्रकाशत्वात् ।
सत्यं ज्ञानमनन्तं ब्रह्मेत्येतस्य लक्षणं प्रथते ॥ २० ॥

* *i.e.,* Unreal.

Brahman, although not knowable (by
the intellect), is yet not unrealisable, because it is self-resplendent. The passage,
"Brahman is reality, knowledge, infinity,"
expresses the definition thereof.   (20)

सति कोशशक्त्युपाधौ सम्भवतस्तस्य जीवतेश्वरते ।
नो चेत्तयोरभावात् विगतविशेषं विभाति निजरूपम् ॥

As long as there is limitation by the
powers of the sheaths, the conditions of
individual soul and Supreme Self affect
it. Otherwise, these two conditions disappear, and its real nature without any
distinction shines forth.   (21)

सति सकलदृश्यबाधे न किमप्यस्तीति लोकसिद्धं चेत् ।
यन्न किमपीति सिद्धं ब्रह्म तदेवेति वेदतः सिद्धम् ॥

If it is determined by ordinary reasoning that, when everything visible is
known to be unreal, there is naught at
all, it is further determined by the Vedas
that what is established as naught at all,
is Brahman itself.   (22)

एकमपि विरहितानां तत्त्वमसीयादिवाक्यचिन्तनया ।
प्रतिभात्येष परोक्षवदात्मा प्रत्यक्प्रकाशमानोऽपि ॥२३॥

Although this is so, to those that are devoid of even a thought of passages like "that thou art," the self, though (ever) resplendent within becomes, as it were, invisible. (23)

तस्मात्पदार्थशोधनपूर्वं वाक्यस्य चिन्तयन्नर्थम् ।
देशिकदयाप्रभावादपरोक्षयति क्षणेन चात्मानम् ॥२४॥

Therefore, by a contemplation of the meaning of such passages through an examination of their word-meanings, and by the glory of the grace of the Master, one directly sees the self in an instant. (24)

देहेन्द्रियादिधर्मान् आत्मन्यारोपयन्नभेदेन ।
कर्तृत्वाद्यभिमानी बोधः स्यात्त्वंपदस्य वाच्योऽर्थः ॥

The expressed meaning of the word 'thou' is the (individual) consciousness that prides in being doer, (enjoyer,) etc., super-imposing the functions of the body, the senses, etc., on the self as if they were identical. (25)

देहस्य चेन्द्रियाणां साक्षी तेभ्यो विलक्षणत्वेन ।
प्रतिभाति योऽवबोधः प्रोक्तोऽसौ त्वंपदस्य लक्ष्योऽर्थः ॥

The derived meaning of the word 'thou' is the consciousness that manifests itself

as the witness of the body, the ego, and
the senses, distinct from them.   (26)

वेदावसानवाचा संवेद्यं सकलजगदुपादानम् ।
सर्वज्ञताद्युपेतं चैतन्यं तत्पदस्य वाच्योऽर्थः ॥ २७ ॥

The expressed meaning of the word
"that" is the supreme self which is knowable from Vedantic texts, which is the
efficient cause of the whole universe, and
which is endowed with omniscience, etc.
                                              (27)

विविधोपाधिविमुक्तं विश्वातीतं विशुद्धमद्वैतम् ।
अक्षरमनुभववेद्यं चैतन्यं तत्पदस्य लक्ष्योऽर्थः ॥२८॥

The derived   meaning of the word
"that" is the supreme self, free of all condition whatsoever, beyond all phenomena, absolute, secondless, external, and
realisable by (direct) experience.   (28)

सामानाधिकरण्यं तदनु विशेषणविशेष्यता चेति ।
अथ लक्ष्यलक्षकत्वं भवति पदार्थान्तमनां च सम्बन्धः ॥

The relation between the two word-
meanings is either sameness of object,
or the relation of attribute and subject, or
that of indicated and indicator.   . (29)

एकत्र वृत्तिरर्थे शब्दानां भिन्नवृत्तिहेतूनाम् ।
सामानाधिकरण्यं भवतीत्येवं वदन्ति लाक्षणिकाः ॥

Those versed in interpretation explain "sameness of object" as the application of words, individually denoting different objects, to denote together the same object. (30)

प्रात्यक्ष्यं पारोक्ष्यं परिपूर्णत्वं च सद्वितीयत्वम् ।
इतरेतरं विरुद्धं तत इह भवितव्यमेव लक्षणया ॥३१॥

Visibility and invisibility, fullness and the having a second, are mutually contradictory. Therefore, in the case on hand, the derived meaning alone is possible. (31)

मानान्तरोपरोधे मुख्यार्थस्यापरिग्रहे जाते ।
मुख्याविनाकृतेऽर्थे या वृत्तिः सैव लक्षणा प्रोक्ता ॥

Derivation of meaning is the denotation of an object not unconnected with the primary meaning, in a case where the primary meaning cannot be adopted owing to its contradiction by other reasons. (32)

निखिलमपि वाच्यमर्थं यक्त्वा वृत्तिस्तदन्वितेऽन्यार्थे ।
जहतीति लक्षणा स्यात् गङ्गायां घोषवदिह न ग्राह्या ॥

Exclusive derivation of meaning* is the denotation of a different object connect-

---

*Derivation of meaning is of three kinds: exclusive, inclusive, and partly exclusive and partly inclusive.

ed with the expressed meaning, but completely exclusive of the latter; for instance, the hamlet on the Ganges.* Such derivation of meaning is not applicable to the present case. (33)

वाच्यार्थमलयजन्त्याः यस्या वृत्तेः प्रवृत्तिरन्यार्थे ।
इयमजहतीति कथिता शोणो धावतिवदत्र न ग्राह्या ॥

Inclusive derivation of meaning is the denotation of another object without abandoning the expressed meaning; for instance, the red † (one) is running. Such derivation, too, should not be adopted in the present. (34)

जहदजहतीति सा स्यात् या वाच्यार्थैकदेशमपहाय ।
बोधयति चैकदेशं सोऽयं द्विज इतिवदाश्रयेदेनाम् ॥

The partly exclusive and partly inclusive derivation is that which excludes a portion of the expressed object and denotes another portion thereof; for instance, "this is that Brahmin." This mode of derivation should be adopted in the present case. (35)

सोऽयं द्विज इति वाक्यं लत्त्वा प्रत्यक्परोक्षदेशाद्यम् ।
द्विजमात्रलक्षकत्वात् कथयत्यैक्यं पदार्थयोरुभयोः ॥

---

*Which really means "the banks of the Ganges."
†The quality of redness cannot run. The red horse or other animal is meant

The sentence, "this is that Brahmin",
indicates the Brahmin alone by excluding
the remoteness and the nearness of place,
(time), etc., and thus denotes identity
between the meanings of the two words
('this' and 'that').   (36)

तद्वत्तत्त्वमसीति त्वत्तवा प्रत्यक्परोक्षतादीनि ।
चिद्वत्सु लक्षयित्वा बोधयति स्पष्टमसिपदेनैक्यम् ॥

In the same way, the sentence, "that
thou art" indicates the Supreme Self that
is the reality, by excluding directness
and remoteness, etc., and thus clearly
denotes identity* by the word "art." (37)

इत्थं बोधितमर्थं महता वाक्येन दर्शितैक्येन ।
अहमित्यपरोक्षयतां वेदो वेदयति वीतशोकत्वम् ॥

In regard to those that realise as "I"
the reality thus indicated by the principal text declaring identity, the Vedas
declare that they shall be free from all
sorrow.   (38)

प्रायः प्रवर्तकत्वं विधिवचसां लोकवेदयोर्दृष्टम् ।
सिद्धं बोधयतोऽर्थं कथमेतद्ब्रवति तत्त्वमस्यादेः ॥३९॥

_____
*Between the two indicated by "that" and "thou."

It is generally observed, both in secular and Vedic matters that words of injunction (alone) are capable of inciting one to action. How can the same hold good in the case of passages like "that thou art" which (merely) reveal a thing already established? (39)

विधिरेव न प्रवृत्तिं जनयत्यभिलषितवस्तुबोधोऽपि ।
राजा भवति सुतोऽभूत् इति बोधेन प्रवर्तते लोकः ॥

It is not injunction alone that can incite one to action, but also an assertion regarding a desired object. A person will begin to to act by virtue of the knowledge. "Here is the king" or "a son has been born." (40)

ऐक्यपरैः श्रुतिवाक्यैः आत्मा शश्वत्प्रकाशमानोऽपि ।
देशिकदयाविहीनैः अपरोक्षयितुं न शक्यते पुरुषैः ॥

Although, according to the Vedic passages declaring identity, the self is incessantly revealed, yet it is not possible to realise it for those that are devoid of the grace of the Master. (41)

विरहितकाम्यनिषिद्धो विहितानुष्ठाननिर्मलखान्तः ।
भजति स्वमेव बोधं गुरुणा किमिति त्वया न मन्तव्यम् ॥

Do not think, 'what is the need for a
Master, since one, by himself, can attain
a knowledge of the self by avoiding
optional and prohibited rites and by
purifying the mind through the performance of prescribed rites ?'   (42)

कर्मभिरेव न बोधः प्रभवति गुरुणा विना दयानिधिना ।
आचार्यवान्हि पुरुषो वेदेत्यर्थस्य वेदसिद्धत्वात् ॥४३॥

Knowledge (of self) cannot result from
rites alone, without the Master that is the
ocean of mercy; for it is established by
the Vedas that only he who has a Master
can know.   (43)

वेदोऽनादितया वा यद्वा परमेश्वरप्रणीततया ।
भवति परमं प्रमाणं बोधो नास्ति स्वतश्च परतो वा ॥

The Vedas are the highest authority,
either because they are beginningless or
because they are the utterances of the
Supreme Lord. Knowledge, (therefore,)
cannot result either by itself or from any
other authority.   (44)

नापेक्षते यदन्यत् यदपेक्षन्तेऽखिलानि मानानि ।
वाक्यं तन्निगमानां मानं ब्रह्माद्यतीन्द्रियावगतौ ॥४५॥

The Vedic sentence, which does not
depend on any other proof, but on which

depend all proofs, is the only source of
the knowledge of Brahman and other
things that are beyond the senses.   (45)

मानं प्रबोधयन्तं बोधं मानेन ये बुभुत्सन्ते ।
एधोभिरेव दहनं दग्धुं वाञ्छन्ति ते महात्मानः ॥४६॥

Those that attempt, by means of proof,
to realise a knowledge which reveals the
proof itself, are such wonderful beings
that they will burn fire itself by means of
fuel.   (46)

वेदोऽनादिरमुष्य व्यञ्जक ईशस्स्वयंप्रकाशात्मा ।
तदभिव्यक्तिमुदीक्ष्य प्रोक्तोऽसौ सूरिभिः प्रमाणमिति ।

The Veda is beginningless, and the
self-resplendent Lord himself manifests
it. In view of its manifestation, thus the
great ones have declared that it is the
(highest) authority.   (47)

रूपाणामवलोके चक्षुरिवान्यन्न कारणं दृष्टम् ।
तद्वददृष्टावगतौ वेदवदन्यो न वेदको हेतुः ॥ ४८ ॥

As no authority is equal to the eye in
the perception of forms, so is there no
authority for knowledge, equal to the
Veda, in the realisation of that which is
beyond perception.   (48)

निगमेषु निश्चितार्थं तन्त्रे कश्चिद्यदि प्रकाशयति ।
तदिदमनुवादमात्रं प्रामाण्यं तस्य सिध्यति न किञ्चित् ॥

If any treatise elucidates a truth established by the Vedas, it is merely a repetition and is not indicative of any authority whatsoever.   (49)

अंशद्वयवति निगमे साधयति द्वैतमेव कोऽप्यंशः ।
अद्वैतमेव वस्तु प्रतिपादयति प्रसिद्धमपरोंऽशः ॥५०॥

Of the Vedas consisting of the parts,
one part* enunciates duality and the
other† plainly expounds the one (secondless) reality.   (50)

अद्वैतमेव सत्यं तस्मिन्द्वैतं न सत्यमध्यस्तम् ।
रजतमिव शुक्तिकायां मृगतृष्णायामिवोदकस्फुरणम् ॥

The secondless alone is real. Duality,
being only superimposed thereon, is not
real, like (the illusion of) silver in the
mother-o'-pearl, or the appearance of
water in a mirage.   (51)

आरोपितं यदि स्यात् अद्वैतं वस्त्ववस्तुनि द्वैते ।
युक्तं नैव तदा स्यात् सत्येऽध्यासो भवत्यसत्यानाम् ॥

It is not proper to say that the secondless reality may be superimposed on the

---

* The *karma-kanda*.   † The *jnana-kanda*.

unreal and dual ; for superimposition is
(always) that of the unreal on the real.

(52)

यद्यारोपणमुभयोः तद्व्यतिरिक्तस्य कस्यचिदभावात् ।
आरोपणं न शून्ये तस्मादद्वैतसत्यता ग्राह्या   ॥ ५३ ॥

Both cannot be superimposed, for there
is naught different from them and superimposition cannot be on nothing. Hence,
the reality of the secondless (self) must
be accepted.   (53)

प्रत्यक्षादनवगतं श्रुत्वा प्रतिपादनीयमद्वैतम् ।
द्वैतं न प्रतिपाद्यं तस्य स्वयमेव लोकसिद्धत्वात् ॥५४॥

What is expounded by the Vedas is
the secondless (Brahman) that cannot be
known by direct perception and other
proofs, and not duality for the latter is
already established by ordinary reason_
ing.   (54)

अद्वैतं सुखरूपं दुस्सहदुःखं सदा भवेद्द्वैतम् ।
यत्र प्रयोजनं स्यात् प्रतिपादयति श्रुतिस्तदेवासौ ॥

The secondless (Brahman) is of the
nature of happiness, while duality is
always unendurable misery. The Vedas,
therefore, expound only that* which is
aspired for.   (55)

निगमगिरा प्रतिपाद्यं वस्तु यदानन्दरूपमद्वैतम् ।
स्वाभाविकस्वरूपं जीवत्वं तस्य केचन ब्रुवते ॥ ५६ ॥

---

* Brahman, that is, eternal bliss.

In respect of the secondless reality
which is expounded by the Vedas and
which is of the nature of bliss, some say
that the condition of individual self is its
ordinary nature. (56)

स्वाभाविकं यदि स्यात् जीवत्वं तस्य विशदविज्ञप्तेः ।
सकृदपि न तद्विनाशं गच्छेदुष्णप्रकाशवद्दृढेः ॥ ५७ ॥

If the condition of individual self be
the very nature of (Brahman that is) absolute consciousness, then, like the heat
and light of fire, it can never disappear.
(57)

यद्धृदयो रसविद्धं काञ्चनतां याति तद्वदेवासौ ।
जीवस्साधनशक्त्या परतां यातीति केचिदिच्छन्ति ॥

Some are of opinion that the individual
soul becomes the supreme soul by virtue
of spiritual effort in the same way as iron
becomes gold by the action of some
chemical. (58)

तदिदं भवति न युक्तं गतवति तस्मिन्श्चिरेण रसवीर्ये ।
प्रतिपद्यते प्रणाशं हैमो वर्णोऽप्ययस्समारूढः ॥ ५९ ॥

This is not right; for when the power
of the chemical disappears by lapse of
time, the golden colour that was imparted
to the iron, also disappears. (59)

जीवत्वमपि तथेदं बहुविधसुखदुःखलक्षणोपेतम् ।
गतमिव साधनशक्तथा प्रतिभात्येव प्रयाति न
[विनाशम् ॥ ६० ॥

In the same way, the condition of individual soul, with its characteristics of
pleasure and pain, will only seem to disappear (according to the above reasoning), but will not be utterly destroyed.
(60)

तस्मात्स्वतो यदि स्यात् जीवस्ततं स एव जीवः स्यात् ।
एवं यदि परमात्मा परमात्मैवायमिति भवेद्युक्तम् ॥

Therefore, if, by its very nature, it is
the individual self, it will for ever remain
the individual self. In the same way, if
(by its very nature) it is the supreme self,
it stands to reason that it is always the
supreme self.   (61)

यदि वा परेण साम्यं जीवश्चेद्भजति साधनबलेन ।
कालेन तदपि कियता नश्यत्येवेति निश्चितं सकलैः ॥

Even if the individual soul were to
attain (only a) similarity with the supreme self by virtue of spiritual efforts, it
has been decided by all authorities that
even that similarity must necessarily
perish after some time*.   (62)

---

* Because whatever has an artificial origin must
have an end.

तस्मात्परं स्वकीयं मोहं मोहात्मकं च संसारम् ।
स्वज्ञानेन जहित्वा पूर्णः स्वयमेव शिष्यते नान्यत् ॥

Having therefore destroyed, by the
knowledge of the self, the insuperable
ignorance regarding one's self and phenomenal limitation (*samsara*) which is of
(that) ignorance, one becomes oneself the
Infinite, and naught else remains.   (63)

सत्यज्ञानानन्दं प्रकृतं परमात्मरूपमद्वैतम् ।
अवबोधयन्ति निखिलाः श्रुतयः स्मृतिभिः समं
                    [समस्ताभिः ॥ ६४ ॥

All the Vedas and all religious treatises
(*smriti*) expound the supreme secondless
Self whose nature is reality, knowledge
and bliss as the thing to be realised. (64)

एकत्वबोधकानां निखिलानां निगमवाक्यजालानाम् ।
वाक्यान्तराणि सकलान्यभिधीयन्ते स्म शेषभूतानि ॥

In respect of all the numerous Vedic
passages declaring oneness, all other passages are said to be subordinate thereto.
                                    (65)

यस्मिन्निहिरवदुदितेतिमिरवदपयान्ति कर्तृताऽऽदीनि
ज्ञानं विरहितभेदं कथमेतद्ब्रवति तत्त्वमस्यादेः ॥६६॥

*From passages like "that thou art,"
how does the knowledge of non-duality
spring up, at whose very origin the conditions of doer, etc., disappear, like darkness at the rise of the sun?　(66)

कर्मप्रकरणनिष्ठं ज्ञानं कर्माङ्गमिष्यते प्राज्ञैः ।

भिन्नप्रकरणभाजः कर्माङ्गत्वं कथं भवेज्ज्ञमेः ॥ ६७ ॥

Those versed in ritual argue that knowledge occurs in the ritual portion (of the
Veda) and is therefore an auxiliary to
ritual. But how can knowledge be an
auxiliary to ritual, since it occurs in a
quite different context?　(67)

अधिकारिविषयभेदौ कर्मज्ञानात्मकावुभौ काण्डौ ।

एवं सति कथमनयोरङ्गाङ्गित्वं परस्परं घटते ॥ ६८ ॥

The two portions (of the Veda) relating
to ritual and knowledge, are entirely
different, both in respect of the aspirant's
qualifications and the subject dealt with.
This being so, how can they be principal
and auxiliary in relation to each other?

(68)

ज्ञानं कर्मणि न स्यात् ज्ञाने कर्मेदमपि तथा न स्यात् ।

कथमनयोरुभयोस्तत् तपनतमोवत्समुच्चयो घटते ॥ ६९ ॥

---

* This and the first half of the next verse are the
view of the *mimamsaka* or ritual school.

Knowledge cannot exist in ritual. So, too, ritual cannot exist in knowledge. How is any correlation possible between the two, which are like sun and darkness? (69)

तस्मान्मोहनिवृत्तौ ज्ञानं न सहायमन्यदर्थयते ।
यद्द्धूनतरतिमिरप्रकरपरिध्वंसने सहस्रांशुः ॥ ७० ॥

Therefore, for the removal of illusion, knowledge does not need the assistance of anything else, in the same way as the sun for the dispulsion of the densest darkness. (70)

ज्ञानं तदेवममलं साक्षी विश्वस्य भवति परमात्मा ।
सम्बध्यते न धर्मैः साक्षी तैरेव सच्चिदानन्दः ॥ ७१ ॥

The supreme self that is the witness of all, is itself that unsullied knowledge. The witness, therefore, is not affected by those limitations (of ignorance) but is (even) reality, knowledge and bliss. (71)

रज्ज्वादेरुरगाद्यैः सम्बन्धवदस्य दृश्यसम्बन्धः ।
सततमसङ्गोऽयमिति श्रुतिरप्यमुमर्थमेव साधयति ७२

Its relation to them as (subject and) object is (illusory) like the relation of rope, etc., to serpent, etc. The Vedas, too

establish the same truth by declaring
"this (self) is ever unattached."   (72)

कर्तृ च कर्म च यस्य स्फुरति ब्रह्मैव तन्न जानाति ।
यस्य न कर्तृ न कर्म स्फुटतरमयमेव वेदितुं क्रमते ॥

That which cognises both subject and
object is the supreme self itself. Neither
of them can know it. That which is
neither subject nor object can alone
know (itself) clearly.   (73)

कर्तृत्वादिकमेतत् मायाशक्त्या प्रतीयते निखिलम् ।
इति केचिदाहुरेषा भ्रान्तिर्ब्रह्मातिरेकतो नान्यत् ॥७४॥

Some say that the nature of doer, (enjoyer) etc. and all else is manifested (in
the self) by its power of *maya*. This is
(however) a delusion, because there is
naught other than Brahman.   (74)

तस्मिन्ब्रह्मणि विदिते विश्वमशेषं भवेदिदं विदितम् ।
कारणमृदि विदितायां घटकरकाद्या यथाऽवगम्यन्ते ॥

That Brahman being known, all this
universe will become known, in the same
way as all earthern jars, pots, etc., become
known by the clay, which is their cause,
being known.   (75)

तदिदं कारणमेकं विगतविशेषं विशुद्धचिद्रूपम् ।
तस्मात्सदेकरूपात् मायोपहिताद्भूदशेषमिदम् ॥७६॥

This (Brahman), then, is the one cause,
devoid of all distinction, of the nature of
purest consciousness. From that which
is the sole reality, conditioned by *maya*,
sprang forth all this universe. (76)

कारणमसदिति केचित् कथयन्त्यसतो भवेन्न कारणता ।
अङ्कुरजननी शक्तिः सति खलु बीजे समीक्ष्यते सकलैः ॥

Some say that the cause is non-entity.
(But) the non-existent cannot be a cause.
The power to generate a sprout is visible
to all, only if the seed exists. (77)

कारणमसदिति कथयन् वन्ध्यापुत्रेण निर्वहेत्कार्यम् ।
किञ्च मृगतृष्णिकाम्भः पीतबोदन्यां महीयसीं शमयेत् ॥

He who declares the cause to be non-
entity, can manage affairs with the son
of a barren woman and quench intense
thirst by drinking the water of a mirage.
(78)

यस्मान्न सोऽयमसतो वादः सम्भवति शास्त्रयुक्तिभ्याम् ।
तस्मात्सदेव तत्त्वं सर्वेषां भवति कारणं जगताम् ॥

As this doctrine of a non-existent cause
is untenable both according to scripture

reason, it follows that real entity is alone
the cause of all the worlds.   (79)

जगदाकारतयाऽपि प्रथते गुरुशिष्यविग्रहतयाऽपि ।

ब्रह्माद्याकारतया प्रतिभातीदं परात्परं तत्त्वम् ॥ ८० ॥

This reality, higher than the highest
manifests itself as the worlds, also as
teacher and pupil, also as (the fourth-
faced) Brahman and other gods.   (80)

सत्यं जगदिति भानं संसृतये स्यादपक्वचित्तानाम् ।

तस्मादसत्यमेतत् निखिलं प्रतिपादयन्ति निगमान्ताः ॥

For those whose minds are not ripe, the
impression that the world is real will
tend to bondage (of births and deaths.)
Hence, the Vedantas declare all this universe to be unreal.   (81)

परिपक्वमानसानां पुरुषवराणां पुरातनैः सुकृतै: ।

ब्रह्मैवेदं सर्वं जगदिति भूयः प्रबोधयत्येष: ॥ ८२ ॥

On the other hand, to those great persons whose minds have become ripe by
virtue of their past merits, the Vedas
declare that all this universe is Brahman
alone.   (82)

अनवगतकाञ्चनानां भूषणधीरेव भूषणे हैमे ।

एवमविवेकभाजां जगति जनानां न तात्त्विकी

[धिषणा ॥ ८३ ॥

Those that do not realise the gold understand a golden ornament only as an ornament. So, too, those that are devoid of realisation do not perceive the world to be Brahman. (83)

अहमालम्बनसिद्धं कस्य परोक्षं भवेदिदं ब्रह्म ।
तदपि विचारविहीनैः अपरोक्षयितुं न शक्यते मुग्धैः ॥

How can Brahman be unknown to anyone, which is realisable by means of I-ness?* And yet, it is impossible of realisation by the unenquiring ignorant. (84)

अहमिदमिति च मतिभ्यां सततं व्यवहरति सर्वलो-
[कोऽपि ।

प्रथमा प्रतीचि चरमा निवसति वपुरिन्द्रियादि-
[बाह्योर्थे ॥ ८५ ॥

All persons carry on their activities at all times by means of the ideas "I" and "this." Of these, the former relates to the inner self, and the latter to external objects like the body, the senses, etc. (85)

वपुरिन्द्रियादिविषयाऽहंबुद्धिश्चेन्महत्यसौ भ्रान्तिः ।
तद्बुद्धिरतसिन्नित्यध्यासत्वेन शास्यमानत्वात् ॥ ८६ ॥

---

* *i.e.* realisable by the experiences common to all, "I am," "I know," "I feel" etc.

If the idea of "I" springs up in respect of the body, senses etc., it is then a huge delusion; for, delusion is defined as the perception of anything in what is not that thing. (86)

तस्मादशेषसाक्षी परमात्मैवाहमर्थ इत्युचितम् ।
अजडवदेव जडोऽयं सत्सम्बन्धाद्द्रवत्यहङ्कारः ॥८७॥

It therefore stands to reason that ths supreme self that is the witness of all ie alone denoted by the idea "I". This I-ness, although devoid of consciousness, becomes conscious, as it were, by its contact with the self. (87)

तस्मात्सर्ववेशरीरेष्वहमहमित्येव भासते स्पष्टः ।
यः प्रत्ययो विशुद्धः तस्य ब्रह्मैव भवति मुख्योऽर्थः ॥

The direct meaning of the clear and unmixed conception, "I", "I", in all bodies is therefore Brahman alone. (88)

गोशब्दादिव गोत्वं तदपि व्यक्तिः प्रतीयतेऽर्थतया ।
अहमर्थः परमात्मा तद्बुद्धान्या भवत्यहङ्कारः ॥ ८९ ॥

By the word "cow,', the genus 'cow' is primarily meant; but, from the context, a particular cow is also indicated. In the

same way the primary meaning of "I" is
the supreme self, but, by virtue of delusion, becomes ego. (89)

दग्धृत्वादिकमयसः पावकसङ्गेन भासते यद्वत् ।
तद्वच्चेतनसङ्गात् अहमि प्रतिभान्ति कर्तृतादीनि ॥

Just as the power to burn, etc., is
manifest in iron by reason of its contact
with fire, so do the conditions of doer,
(enjoyer) etc,, manifest themselves in the
"I" by reason of its connection with the
self. (90)

देहेन्द्रियादिद्दश्यव्यतिरिक्तं विमलमतुलमद्वैतम् ।
अहमर्थमिति विदित्वा तद्व्यतिरिक्तं न कल्पयेत्किञ्चित् ॥

Having understood the meaning of "I"
to be the pure, transcendental, secondless (self) that is different from the body,
senses and other objects, one should not
attribute any other meaning thereto. (91)

यद्वत्सुखदुःखानां अवयवभेदादनेकता देहे ।
तद्वदिह सत्यभेदेऽप्यनुभववैचित्र्यमात्मनामेषाम् ९२

Just as, in the same body, the pleasures
and pains are numerous in respect of the
various limbs, so, too, there are differences of experiences in respect of these

individual souls, although there is really
no differentiation at all. (92)

किमिदं किमस्य रूपं कथमेतभूदमुष्य को हेतुः ।
इति न कदाऽपि विचिन्त्यं चिन्त्यं मायेति धीमता
[विश्वम् ॥ ९३ ॥

A wise person should never enquire of
the universe, 'what is this', 'what is its
nature', 'how was it born' and 'what is its
cause'. He should merely think of it as
delusion. (93)

दन्तिनि दारुविकारे दारु तिरोभवति सोऽपि तत्रैव ।
जगति तथा परमात्मा परमात्मन्यपि जगत्तिरोधत्ते ॥

The wood is forgotten in the elephant
made of wood, and the elephant in the
wood. *So is the supreme self forgotten
in the universe and the universe in the
self. (94)

आत्ममये महति पटे विविधजगच्चित्रमात्मना
[लिखितम् ।
त्वयमेव केवलमसौ पश्यन्प्रमुदं प्रयाति परमात्मा ॥

On the vast canvas of the self, the self
itself paints the picture of the various

---

* Children treat it as an elephant, and the elderly
as wood. So the wise see only the supreme self and
the ignorant the non-self only.

worlds and the supreme-self itself derives
extreme bliss from seeing that picture.*

(95)

चिन्मात्रममलमक्षयमद्वयमानन्दमनुभवारूढम् ।
ब्रह्मैवास्ति तदन्यत् न किञ्चिदस्तीति निश्चयो विदुषाम्॥

The wise have the firm conviction that
there is nothing else than the supreme
self alone, consisting of pure consciousness, attributeless, imperishable, secondless, of the nature of bliss, and attainable
only by direct realisation.   (96)

व्यवहारस्य दशेयं विद्याऽविद्येति वेदपरिभाषा ।
नास्त्येव तत्त्वदृष्ट्या तत्त्वं ब्रह्मैव नान्यदस्त्यस्मात् ॥

The talk in the Vedas about knowledge
and ne-science relates to the stage of
argumentation. From the   true standpoint there is no such distinction, because
Brahman is the only reality and there is
naught else than this.   (97)

अस्त्यन्यदिति मतं चेत् तदपि ब्रह्मैव चास्तिताऽरूपम् ।
व्यतिरिक्तमस्तितायाः नास्तितया शून्यमेव तत्सिद्धम्॥

If one asserts that there *is* anything
other than the self, even that is the self

---

* As a painter may draw a picture on the back of
his hand and enjoy its sight himself.

in its aspect of existence. Anything
which is different from being existent, is
non-existent and therefore a mere void.

(98)

तत्त्वावबोधशक्त्या स्थिरताया बाधिताऽपि सा माया ।
आदेहपातमेषां आभायात्माऽप्ययं निजो विदुषाम् ॥

For the wise, although delusion has
been conquered by the steady power of
their knowledge of the self, yet it seems
to remain until the death of their bodies.
But the self shines for them in its real
nature.   (99)

एष विशेषो विदुषां पश्यन्तोऽपि प्रपञ्चसंसारम् ।
पृथगात्मनो न किञ्चित् पश्येयुः सकलनिगमनिर्णीतात् ॥

This is the peculiarity of the wise, that,
although they are looking at all the
variety of phenomenal existence, they
could see naught other than the self understood from all the Vedas.   (100)

किं चिन्त्यं किमचिन्त्यं किं कथनीयं किमप्यकथनीयम् ।
किं कृत्यं किमकृत्यं निखिलं ब्रह्मेति जानतां विदुषाम् ॥

For the wise that realise everything to
be Brahman, what is there to meditate or
not medidate, what to speak or not speak,
what to do or not do ?   (101)

निखिलं दृश्यविशेषं दृग्रूपत्वेन पश्यतां विदुषाम् ।
बन्धो नापि न मुक्तिः न परात्मत्वं न चापि जीवत्वम् ॥

For the wise that see all objects as the
self (*drik*), there is neither bondage nor
liberation, neither the condition of supreme self nor that of individual soul. (102)

असकृदनुचिन्तितानां अव्याहततरनिजोपदेशानाम् ।
प्रामाण्यपरमसीम्नां निगमनमिदमेव निखिलनिगमा-
[नाम् ॥ १०३ ॥

This is the sole ultimate teaching of
all the Vedas if they are repeatedly en-
quired into,—the Vedas which uncontra-
dictably reveal the self and which are
the highest authority possible.   (103)

इत्थं निबोध्य गुरुणा शिष्यो हृष्यन्प्रणम्य तं पदयोः ।
स्वानुभवसिद्धमर्थं स्वयमेवान्तर्विचारयामास ॥ १०४ ॥

Thus taught by his master, the disciple
saluted his feet with joy and meditated
within himself on the truth established
by his own direct realisation.   (104)

अजरोऽहमक्षरोऽहं प्राज्ञोऽहं प्रत्यगात्मबोधोऽहम् ।
परमानन्दमयोऽहं परमशिवोऽहं भवामि परिपूर्णः ॥

I am undecaying, I am imperishable,
I am the Lord (*prajna*), I am the consciousness that is the inner self, I am full
of supreme bliss, I am the supreme self
(*parama siva*), I am the infinite.   (105)

आढ्योऽहमात्मभाजां आत्मानन्दानुभूतिरसिकोऽहम् ।
आबालगोपमखिलैः अहमितनुभूयमानमहिमाऽहम् ॥

I am the greatest of those that have realised the self. I am the enjoyer of the
realisation of my own bliss. I am he
whose glory is realised as "I" by all beings down to children and the illiterate.
                                        (106)

इन्द्रियसुखविमुखोऽहं   निजसुखबोधानुभूतिभरितोऽ-
                                        [हम् ।
इतिमतिदूरतरोऽहम् भावेतरसुखितचित्तोऽहम् ॥

I am averse to sensual pleasures. I am
full of the bliss, knowledge and realisation of the self. I am far aloof from any
thought of the objective. I am delighted
at heart by that which is not objective.
                                        (107)

ईशोऽहमीश्वराणां ईर्ष्याद्वेषानुषङ्गरहितोऽहम् ।
ईक्षणविषयमतीनां ईप्सितपुरुषार्थसाधनपरोऽहम् ॥

I am the Lord of Lords. I am devoid
of even a touch of jealousy and hatred.

I am he that fulfils the desired object for
those who are bent on realising the goal.
(108)

उद्योऽहमेव जगतां उपनिषदुद्यानकृतविहारोऽहम् ।
उद्वेलशोकसागरशोषणबाडवहुतवहार्चिरहम् ॥ १०९ ॥

I alone am the origin of the words. I
am he that sports in the garden of the
Upanishads. I am the flame of the sub-
marine fire that will dry up the overflow-
ing ocean of sorrow. (109)

ऊर्जस्खलनिजविभवैः ऊर्ध्वमधस्तिर्यगनुवानोऽहम् ।
ऊहापोहविचारैः उररीकृतवत्प्रतीयमानोऽहम् ॥११०॥

I pervade up and down and around with
my own extraordinary glories. I am he
who appears to be determined by means
of argument, counter argument and enquiry. (110)

ऋषिरहमृषिगणकोऽहं सृष्टिरहं सृज्यमानमहमेव ।
ऋद्धिरहं वृद्धिरहं तृप्तिरहं तृप्तिदीपदीप्तिरहम् ॥१११ ॥

I am the seer. I am the host of seers. I
am the act of creation and I myself am
the created. I am prosperity, I am progress, I am satisfaction, I am the glow of
the lamp of satisfaction. (111)

एकोऽहमेतदीदृशमेवमिति स्फुरितभेदरहितोऽहम् ।
एष्टव्योऽहमनीहैः अन्तःसुकृतानुभूतिरहितोऽहम् ॥

I am one. I am devoid of all distinctions, such as "this," "like this" or
"thus." I am he that should be worship-
ped by the non-desirous. I am devoid of
the inner feeling of merit or demerit.

(112)

ऐक्यावभासकोऽहं वाक्यपरिज्ञानपावनमतीनाम् ।
ऐशमहमेव तत्त्वं नैशतमःप्रायमोहमिहिरोऽहम् ॥

I am the revealer of oneness. I alone
am the supreme reality for minds purified
by a thorough understanding of the
(Vedantic) formula. I am the sun that
dispels ignorance like the darkness of
the night.   (113)

ओजोऽहमोषधीनां ओतप्रोतायमानभुवनोऽहम् ।
ओंकारसारसोल्लसदात्मसुखामोदमत्तभृङ्गोऽहम् ॥

I am the efficacy of herbs, I am the warp
and woof of the worlds. I am the bee in-
toxicated with the fragrance of the bliss
of self emanating from the lotus of the
sacred syllable *Om*.   (114)

औषधमहमशुभानां औपाधिकधर्मजालरहितोऽहम् ।
औदार्यातिशयोऽहं विविधचतुर्वर्गगतारणपरोऽहम् ॥

I am the healing balm for evils. I am
devoid of all conditional properties. I
am the acme of liberality. I am he that
rescues all by (granting) the fourfold
desires* in various ways.   (115)

अङ्कुशमहमखिलानां महत्तया मत्तवारणेन्द्राणाम् ।
अम्बरमिव विमलोऽहं शम्बररिपुजातविकृतिरहितोऽ-
[हम् ॥ ११६ ॥

I am the goad of all powerfullest elephants, being greater than them. I am
as spotless as space. I am devoid of
emotions generated by the god of love.
                                        (116)

आत्मविकल्पमतीनां अस्खलदुपदेशगम्यमानोऽहम् ।
अस्थिरसुखविमुखोऽहं सुस्थिरसुखबोधसम्पदुचितोऽ-
[हम् ॥ ११७ ॥

Amidst doubts and doctrines regarding
the self, I am he that is realised by uner-
ring instruction. I am averse to transient
pleasures. I am fittest for the plenitude
of eternal bliss and knowledge.   (117)

करुणारसभरितोऽहं कबलितकमलासनादिलोकोऽहम् ।
कलुषाहंरहितोऽहं कल्मषमुक्तोपलेपरहितोऽहम् ॥

Dharma, merit. *artha*. riches. *kama*, pleasure and
moksha, liberation.

I am filled with the nectar of mercy. I am he that devours all the worlds including that of the lotus-seated.* I am devoid of the sinful "I". I am free from the contagion of sin and virtue. (118)

खानामगोचरोऽहं खातीतोऽहं खपुष्पभवगोऽहम् ।
खलजनदुरासदोऽहं खण्डज्ञानापनोदनपरोऽहम् ॥

I am beyond the scope of the senses. I transcend the ether (*akasa*). I pervade phenomenal existence which is (unreal) like a skyflower. I am unattainable by the wicked. I am bent on dispelling imperfect knowledge. (119)

गलितद्वैतकथोऽहं गेहीभवदखिलमूलहृदयोऽहम् ।
गन्तव्योऽहमनीहैः गतागतिरहितपूर्णबोधोऽहम् ॥

The very mention of duality will slip away from me. I am he whose dwelling is the innermost heart of all. I am attainable by the contented. I am the perfect consciousness that knows no going or coming. (120)

घनतरविमोहतिमिरप्रकरध्वंसभानुनिकरोऽहम् ।
घटिकावासररजनीवत्सरयुगकल्पकालभेदोऽहम् ॥

* The four-faced Brahma.

I am a host of suns for destroying the accumulated darkness of densest delusion. I am the various divisions of time, hour, day, night, year. *yuga* and *kalpa*.

(121)

चरदचरदात्मकोऽहं चतुरमतिश्लाघ्यचरितोऽहम् ।
चपलजनदुगैंमोऽहं चञ्चलभवजलधिपारदेशोऽहम् ॥

The sentient and the non-sentient are my forms. My actions are extolled by the wisest. I am inaccessible to the unsteady. My abode is the other shore of the boisterous ocean of phenomenal existence.

(122)

छन्दस्सिन्धुनिगूढज्ञानसुखाह्लादमोदमानोऽहम् ।
छलपदविहितमतीनां छन्नोऽहं शान्तिमार्गगम्योऽहम् ॥

I am elated with the joy of conscious bliss that is hidden down the ocean of the Vedas. I am concealed to those whose minds are fond of deceptive verbiage. I am attainable by the way of peace.

(123)

जलजासनादिगोचरपञ्चमहाभूतमूलभूतोऽहम् ।
जगदानन्दकरोऽहं जन्मजरारोगमरणरहितोऽहम् ॥

I am the root of all objects from the lotus-seated (Brahma) downwards and of the five great elements. I impart bliss to

the worlds. I am free from birth, age,
disease and death. (124)

झंकृतिहुंकृतिशिञ्जितबृंहितमुखविविधनादभेदोऽहम् ।
झटितिघटितात्मवेदनदीपपरिस्फुरितहृदयभवनोऽ-
[हम् ॥ १२५

I am the several varieties of noise like
the buzz, the grunt, the tinkling and the
roar. I am he that illuminates the man-
sion of the heart by the lamp of self-
realisation promptly lit. (125)

ज्ञानमहं ज्ञेयमहं ज्ञाताऽहं ज्ञानसाधनगणोऽहम् ।
ज्ञातृज्ञानज्ञेयविनाकृतमस्तित्त्वमात्रमेवाहम् ॥ १२६ ॥

I am knowledge. I am the known. I
am the knower. I am all the aids to knowledge. I am that pure sole existence
bereft of knower, knowledge and known.
(126)

तत्त्वातीतपदोऽहं तदन्तरोऽस्मीतिभावरहितोऽहम् ।
तामसदुरधिगमोऽहं तत्त्वंपदबोधबोध्यहृदयोऽहम् ॥

My nature is beyond all principles. I
am devold of the thought that I am
among them. I am difficult of attainment for the ignorant. My secret is realisable by a knowledge of the words "that"
and "thou." (127)

देवतदैत्यनिशाचरमानवतिर्यङ्महीधरादिरहम् ।
देहेन्द्रियरहितोऽहं दक्षिणपूर्वादिदिग्विभागोऽहम् ॥

I am the foremost of all deities, demons, fiends, men, animals and mountains. I am without body and senses. I
am the various directions like south,
east, etc. (128)

धर्माधर्ममयोऽहं धर्माधर्मादिबन्धरहितोऽहम् ।
धार्मिकजनसुलभोऽहं धन्योऽहं धातुरादिभूतोऽहम् ॥

I am of the nature of right and wrong
I am free from the bondage of right and
wrong etc. I am easily attainable by
those that follow the right. I am the
happiest. I am the origin of the Creator
himself. (129)

नामादिविरहितोऽहं नरकस्वर्गापवर्गरहितोऽहम् ।
नादान्तवेदितोऽहं नानागमनिखिलविश्वसारोऽहम् ॥

I am devoid of names (and forms) etc.
I am free from hell, heaven and liberation. I am he that is realised by the
ultimate inner sound. I am the essence
of all the Vedas and of the whole universe. (130)

परजीवभेदबाधकपरमार्थज्ञानशुद्धचित्तोऽहम् ।
प्रकृतिरहं विकृतिरहं परिणतिरहमसि भागधेयानाम् ॥

I am he whose mind is purified by the
knowledge of the reality which dispels
the distinction between the supreme self
and the individual soul. I am the original. I am the change. I am the fruition
of all fortunes.   (131)

फणधरभूधरवारणविग्रहविधृतप्रपञ्चसारोहम् ।
फालतलोदितलोचनपावकपरिभूतपञ्चबाणोहम् ॥१३२॥

In the shape of the serpent, the moun-
tain and the elephant, I bear the whole
weight of the world. I (am Siva who)
destroyed the five-arrow (Cupid) by the
fire emanating from the eye in the fore-
head.   (132)

बद्धो भवामि नाहं बन्धान्मुक्तस्तथाऽपि नैवाहम् ।
बोध्यो भवामि नाहं बोधोऽहं नैव बोधको नाहम् ॥

I never become bound. So, too, I am
never liberated from bondage. I am
never such as to be taught. I am not the
teaching. I am not the teacher.   (133)

भक्तिरहं भजनमहं मुक्तिरहं मुक्तियुक्तिरहमेव ।
भूतानुशासनोऽहं भूतभवद्व्यमूलभूतोऽहम् ॥१३४॥

I am devotion. I am worship. I am
liberation. I alone am the means to libe-

ration. I am the ruler of all beings. I
am the root-cause of all that is past, present and future.   (134)

मान्योऽहमस्मि महतां मन्दमतीनाममाननीयोहम् ।
मदरागमानमोहितमानसदुर्वासनादुरापोहम् ॥ १३५ ॥

I am respected by the great. I am dis-
respected by the ignorant. I am difficult
to attain, owing to the evil tendencies of
the mind deluded by pride, desire and
vanity.   (135)

यजनयजमानयाजकयागमयोहं यमादिरहितोहम् ।
यमवरुणयक्षवासवराक्षसमरुदीशवह्निरूपोहम् ॥

I am the sacrificial rite, the sacrificer,
the priest and the sacrifice. I am free
from control of mind etc.* I am Yama,
Varuna, Kubera, Indra, Nirriti, Vayu,
Isvara and Agni.†   (136)

रक्षाविधानशिक्षावीक्षितलीलावलोकमहिमाहम् ।
रजनीदिवसविरामस्फुरदनुभूतिप्रमाणसिद्धोहम् ॥

I am the glory of that playful glance
that affords protection and witnesses the

---

* The eight limbed (or Raja—) Yoga.
† The eight deities presiding over the eight cardinal
points.

control (of the universe.) I am established by the authority of that realisation
which springs up amidst conditions
wherein there is neither night nor day.

(137)

लक्षणलक्ष्यमयोहं लाक्षणिकोहं लयादिरहितोहम् ।
लाभालाभमयोहं लब्धव्यानामलभ्यमानोहम् ॥१३८॥

I am the definition and the defined. I
am the implied meaning. I am devoid of
dissolution etc. I am the gain and the
loss. I am the unattained amidst the
attainable.

(138)

वर्णाश्रमरहितोहं वर्णमयोहं वरेण्यगण्योहम् ।
वाचामगोचरोहं वचसामर्थे पदे निविष्टोहम् ॥१३९॥

I have no castes or rules of life. I am
the sacred syllables. I am the respected
among the most respectable. I am beyond
the scope of speech. I am within the
words and the meaning of every sentence.

(139)

शमदमविरहितमनसां शास्त्रशतैरप्यगम्यमानोहम् ।
शरणमहमेव विदुषां शकलीकृतविविधसंशयगणोहम् ॥

I am unattainable even by hundreds of
philosophies for minds that are devoid of
peace and self-control. I am the sole

refuge of the wise. I break to pieces
countless doubts of various sorts.   (140)

षड्भावविरहितोहं षड्गुणरहितोहमहितरहितोहम् ।
षट्कोशविरहितोहं षट्त्रिंशत्तत्त्वजालरहितोहम् ॥

I am free from the six states* and the
six tastes.† I have no enemy. I am free
from the six bodily sheaths.‡ I am beyond the thirty-six principles.§   (141)

संवित्सुखात्मकोहं समाधिसंकल्पकल्पवृक्षोहम् ।
संसारविरहितोहं साक्षात्कारोऽहमात्मविद्यायाः॥१४२॥

I am the bliss of realisation. I am the
celestial tree that grants the desire for
absorbed contemplation. I am free from
phenomenal condition. I am the direct
realisation of the Vedanta (*atma vidya*)
(142)

हव्यमहं कव्यमहं हेयोपादेयभावशून्योहम् ।
हरिरहमस्मि हरोहं विधिरहमेवास्मि कारणं तेषाम् ॥

---

*Birth; existence, growth. ripeness, decay, death.
†Sweet, sour. salt, bitter, pungent and astringent.
‡Skin muscles, blood, nerves. bones and marrow.
§The five elements, the five pranas (vital breaths).
the five sensory and the five motor organs, the four
aspects of the mind, *mahat, kala,* (time), *pradhana,
maya, avidya, purusha, bindu, nada, sakti, siva, santa.*
and *atita.*

I am the oblation to the gods and the oblation to the *manes.* I am devoid of all ideas of rejection and acceptance. I am Vishnu, I am Siva, I am Brahman (the creator), and I alone am their cause. (143)

क्षालितकलुषमयोहं क्षपितभवक्लेशजालहृदयोहम् ।
क्षान्ताद्यक्षरसुघटितविविधव्यवहारमूलमहमेव ॥

All my sins have been washed away. The sorrows of phenomenal existence have been dispelled from my heart. I am the root of all the various activities expressed by the letters ending with *ksha* and beginning with *a.*＊   (144)

बहुभिः किमेभिरुक्तैः अहमेवेदं चराचरं विश्वम् ।
शीकरफेनतरङ्गाः सिन्धोरपराणि न खलु वस्तूनि ॥

Why say so much! All this universe, sentient and non-sentient, is myself. Spray and foam and wave are not, in reality, substances different from the ocean.   (145)

शरणं न हि मम जननी
न पिता न सुता न सोदरा नान्ये ।
परमं शरणमिदं स्यात्
चरणं मम मूर्ध्नि देशिकन्यस्तम् ॥ १४६ ॥

＊ अ *(a)* and क्ष *(ksha)* are the first and last letters of the Samskrit alphabet.

My refuge is neither my mother, nor
father, nor sons, nor others. My supreme refuge shall be the foot placed by
my master on my head.   (146)

आस्ते देशिकचरणं निरवधिरास्ते तदीक्षणे करुणा ।
आस्ते किमपि यदुक्तं किमतःपरमस्ति जन्मसाफल्यम्॥

There is the foot of the master. There
is unbounded mercy in his look. There
is whatever he has taught. Is there any
higher fulfilment of life?   (147)

हिमकरकरौघसान्द्राः कांक्षितवरदानकल्पकविशेषाः ।
श्रीगुरुचरणकटाक्षाः शिशिराश्शमयन्ति चित्तसन्ता-
             [पम् ॥ ॥१४८ ॥

The looks of the venerable master are
as full as the flood of rays of the (full)
moon, they are a variety of the celestial
tree in granting whatever boon is desired,
and they soothen and quell the sorrow of
the mind.   (148)

कबलितचञ्चलचेतोगुरुतरमण्डूकजातपरितोषा ।
शेते हृद्यगुहायां चिरतरमेकैव चिन्मयी भुजगी ॥

In the cave of the heart there lies for
ever by herself, the serpent-maid of pure

consciousness, made happy by swallow-
ing the huge frog of a fickle mind.   (149)

मयि सुखबोधपयोधौ महति ब्रह्माण्डबुद्बुदसहस्रम् ।
मायाविशेषशालिनि भूत्वा भूत्वा पुनस्तिरोधत्ते ॥

In the vast ocean of bliss and realisation, which is myself, characterised by
maya, a thousand universe-bubbles spring
up and disappear again and again.   (150)

गुरुकृपयैव सुनावा प्राक्तनभाग्यप्रवृद्धमारुतया ।
दुस्सहदुःखतरङ्गः तुङ्गः संसारसागरस्तीर्णः ॥ १५१ ॥

Solely by the good ship of the master's
grace, wafted by the wind of good luck
acquired in former lives, I have crossed
the vast ocean of phenomenal existence,
whose waves of sorrow are unendurable.
(151)

सति तमसि मोहरूपे विश्वमपश्यं तदेतदित्यखिलम् ।
उदितवति बोधभानौ किमपि न पश्यामि किं त्विदं
[चित्रम् ॥ १५१ ॥

While there was the darkness of ignorance, I saw the whole universe as a reality before my eyes. But when the sun of

knowledge has risen, I see nothing at
all. This is wonderful !   (152)

नाहं नमामि देवान् देवानतीत्य न सेवते देवम् ।
न तदनु करोति विधानं तस्मै यतते नमो नमो मह्यम् ॥

I prostrate not to the gods. One who
is beyond all gods not salute a god. After
that stage, one does no prescribed act. I
prostrate again and again to my own
self, which is the root of all endeavour.
                                              (153)

इत्यात्मबोधलाभं मुहुरप्यनुचिन्त्य मोदमानेन ।
प्रारब्धकर्मणोऽन्ते परं पदं प्राप्यते स कैवल्यम् ॥

Thus, rejoicing again and again at the
thought of his having gained the knowledge of the self, he reaches the supreme
state of absolutenss (*kaivalya*), when the
fruits of actions ripe for present enjoyment are exhausted.   (154)

मोहान्धकारहरणं संसारोद्वेलसागरोत्तरणम् ।
स्वात्मनिरूपणमेतत् प्रकरणमकुरुत दक्षिणामूर्तिः ॥

The Lord facing the south*, himself,
has composed this work entitled " The

---
* Dakshinamurti, the Lord Siva in the shape of a
spiritual teacher.

definition of one's own self", which will dispel the darkness of ignorance and will carry one across the shoreless ocean of phenomenal existence.   (155)

अज्ञानान्ध्यविहन्ता विरचितविज्ञानपङ्कजोल्लासः ।
मानसगगनतलं मे भासयति श्रीनिवासगुरुभानुः ॥

The sky of my mind is illumined by the sun of the master who is the Lord Vishnu that destroys the darkness of ignorance and causes the lotus of realisation to blossom.   (156)

Here Ends
The Definition of One's Own Self.

———

MISCELLANEOUS STOTRAS

REPRINT FROM

" PRAYERS, PRAISES AND PSALMS "

॥ आचार्यकृतस्तोत्राणि ॥

❧

गभीरे कासारे विशति विजने घोरविपिने
विशाले शैले न भ्रमति कुसुमार्थं जडमतिः ।
समर्प्यैकं चेतस्सरसिजमुमानाथ भवते
सुखेनावस्थातुं जन इह न जानाति किमहो ॥

हंसः पद्मवनं समिच्छति यथा नीलाम्बुदं चातकः
कोकः कोकनदप्रियं प्रतिदिनं चन्द्रं चकोरस्तथा ।
चेतो वाञ्छति मामकं पशुपते चिन्मार्गमृग्यं विभो
गौरीनाथ भवत्पदाब्जयुगलं कैवल्यसौख्यप्रदम् ॥

अङ्कोलं निजबीजसन्ततिरयस्कान्तोपलं सूचिका
साध्वी नैजविभुं लता क्षितिरुहं सिन्धुस्सरिद्वल्लभम् ।
प्राप्नोतीह यथा तथा पशुपतेः पादारविन्दद्वयं
चेतोवृत्तिरुपेत्य तिष्ठति सदा तद् भक्तिरित्युच्यते ॥

The Sivanandalahari 9, 59, 61.

Stupid man enters deep lakes and wanders over lonely and terrible forests and long mountains, in search of flowers. Alas! do not people here know to offer you, O Lord of Uma, the single lotus of their heart and rest in happiness?

Lord of Gauri! as the swan loves the lotus-bed, the Chataka bird, the dark (water-laden) cloud, the Koka bird, the sun every day and the Chakora bird, the moon,—even so, O Lord of beings, my mind desires your lotus-feet, which, sought through the path of knowledge, bestow the happiness of salvation.

As its own seeds reach back the Ankola tree, as a needle is drawn to the magnet, as a chaste wife remains with her own lord, as a creeper clings to the tree, as the river merges in the ocean,— if thought thus reaches the lotus-feet of Lord Pasupati and remains there for all time, that is said to be devotion.

The Sivanandalahari, 9, 59, 61.

न मन्त्रं नो यन्त्रं तदपि च न जाने स्तुतिमहो
 न चाह्वानं ध्यानं तदपि च न जाने स्तुतिकथाः ।
न जाने मुद्रास्ते तदपि च न जाने विलपनं
 परं जाने मातस्त्वदनुसरणं क्लेशहरणम् ॥

विधेरज्ञानेन द्रविणविरहेणालसतया
 विधेयाशक्यत्वात् तव चरणयोर्या च्युतिरभूत् ।
तदेतत्क्षन्तव्यं जननि सकलोद्धारिणि शिवे
 कुपुत्रो जायेत क्वचिदपि कुमाता न भवति ॥

 आपत्सु मग्नः स्मरणं त्वदीयं
  करोमि दुर्गे करुणार्णवेशि ।
 नैतच्छठत्वं मम भावयेथाः
  क्षुधातृषार्ता जननीं स्मरन्ति ॥

The Devyaparadhakshamapana Stotra, I, 2, 10.

 यत्रैव यत्रैव मनो मदीयं
  तत्रैव तत्रैव तव स्वरूपम् ।
 यत्रैव यत्रैव शिरो मदीयं
  तत्रैव तत्रैव पद्द्वयं ते ॥

The Tripurasundrai Vedapada Stotra, 10.

I know no Mantra, Yantra or Stotra; I know no invocation or contemplation; I know no stories in your praise; I know not your Mudras, not even how to cry out (to you); simply, I know, Mother, to run after you, which (itself) destroys (all my) distress.

By a mistake of fate, poverty, laziness or the impossibility of becoming your devotee, I have dropped from your feet. Auspicious Mother! Goddess who uplifts all! this must be excused (by you). A bad son may be born; but there is no bad mother anywhere.

Goddess Durga, ocean of compassion, I think of you (only) when I am immersed in calamities; do not take it as roguery on my part; (only) when hungry and thirsty do (children) think of their mother.

The Devyaparadhakshamapana Stotra, 1, 2, 10.

Wherever my mind, there be your form; wherever my head, there be your feet.

The Tripurasundari Vedapada Stotra, 10.

भज गोविन्दं भज गोविन्दं

भज गोविन्दं मूढमते !

संप्राप्ते सन्निहिते काले

न हि न हि रक्षति डुकृञ्करणे ॥

मूढ जहीहि धनागमतृष्णां

कुरु सद्बुद्धिं मनसि वितृष्णाम् ।

यल्लभसे निजकर्मोपात्तं

वित्तं तेन विनोदय चित्तम् ॥

नलिनीदलगतजलमतितरलं

तद्वज्जीवितमतिशयचपलम् ।

विद्धि व्याध्यभिमानग्रस्तं

लोकं शोकहतं च समस्तम् ॥

यावद्वित्तोपार्जनशक्तः

तावन्निजपरिवारो रक्तः ।

पश्चाज्जीवति जर्जरदेहे

वार्तां कोऽपि न गृच्छति गेहे ॥

बालस्तावत्क्रीडासक्तः

तरुणस्तावत्तरुणीसक्तः ।

वृद्धस्तावच्चिन्तासक्तः

परे ब्रह्मणि कोऽपि न सक्तः ॥

Worship Lord Govinda, worship Him, worship Him, you fool! When your appointed time draws near, (your) knowledge of grammar will not save you, never.

Fool! abandon the desire for amassing wealth; cultivate good thoughts in your mind devoid of avarice; the wealth which you get, as a result of your past Karman—please your mind with that.

The water on the lotus-leaf is extremely unsteady; even so is life fickle in the extreme; know that, gripped by disease and desire, the whole world becomes struck with misery.

So long as man is efficient to earn money, those around him are attached to him; if he survives as a decrepit, none will even call at his house to enquire of him.

The boy is immersed in play; the youth, in the youthful damsel; the old, in anxiety; (but) none in the Supreme Being!

कुरुते गङ्गासागरगमनं
व्रतपरिपालनमथवा दानम् ।
ज्ञानविहीनः सर्वमतेन
मुक्तिं न भजति जन्मशतेन ॥

पुनरपि जननं पुनरपि मरणं
पुनरपि जननीजठरे शयनम् ।
इह संसारे बहुदुस्तारे
कृपयाऽपारे पाहि मुरारे ॥

त्वयि मयि चान्यत्रैको विष्णुः
व्यर्थं कुप्यसि मय्यसहिष्णुः ।
सर्वस्मिन्नपि पश्यात्मानं
सर्वत्रोत्सृज भेदाज्ञानम् ॥

गेयं गीतानामसहस्रं
ध्येयं श्रीपतिरूपमजस्रम् ।
नेयं सज्जनसङ्गे चित्तं
देयं दीनजनाय च वित्तम् ॥

The Mohamudgara.

One goes on pilgrimages to the Ganges
and the ocean, keeps vows, or makes
gifts ; (but),—whatever the creed—the
man devoid of knowledge does not obtain
deliverance (even) after a hundred
births.

Birth again, death again and lying
again in the womb of a mother ! O God
Murari ! kindly save (me) from this endless Samsara, so difficult to overcome.

In you, in me and elsewhere also, it is
all one God Vishnu ; in vain do you become intolerant and angry towards me ;
see your Self in everything ; leave off the
nescience of (seeing) difference every-
where.

The 'Gita' and the 'Thousand Names'
of the Lord must be sung ; the form of the
Lord of Goddess Lakshmi (Hari) must be
constantly contemplated ; the mind must
be led to the company of the good and
the possessions (one has) must be given
to the distressed.

The Mohamudgara.

प्रातस्स्मरामि देवस्य
सवितुर्भर्गं आत्मनः ।
वरेण्यं तद्धियो यो नः
चिदानन्दे प्रचोदयात् ॥

The Sadacharanusandhana, 3.

प्रातर्नमामि तमसः परमर्कवर्णं
पूर्णं सनातनपदं पुरुषोत्तमाख्यम् ।
यस्मिन्निदं जगदशेषमशेषमूर्तौ
रज्ज्वां भुजङ्गम इव प्रतिभासितं वै ॥

The Pratassmarana Stotra, 3.

काशीक्षेत्रं शरीरं
त्रिभुवनजननी व्यापिनी ज्ञानगङ्गा,
भक्तिः श्रद्धा गयेयं
निजगुरुचरणध्यानयोगः प्रयागः ।
विश्वेशोऽयं तुरीयं
सकलजनमनस्साक्षिभूतोऽन्तरात्मा
देहे सर्वं मदीये
यदि वसति पुनस्तीर्थमन्यत्किमस्ति ॥

The Kasipanchaka, 5.

I think of, at dawn, the foremost effulgence of my divine and creative Self, that it may direct our (my) mind(s) to the Bliss of Consciousness.

The Sadacharanusandhana, 3.

I bow, in the early morning, to the Full, the Eternal, that sun-hued Purushottama beyond the darkness, in whose all-comprehending form, this entire universe has been made to flash forth, like a snake where there is (only) a rope.

The Pratassmarana Stotra, 3.

This body is the holy place of *Benares*; (and here flows) the all-pervasive *Ganges* of Wisdom, the mother of the three worlds; this devotion and this faith are *Gaya*; the contemplation of the feet of my own perceptor is *Prayaga* (*Allahabad*); this inner self, the Brahman, the witness of the mind of all people, is the God, the Lord of the universe; if everything (thus) abides in myself, is there any other shrine (besides it)?

The Kasipanchaka, 5.

जपो जल्पः शिल्पं सकलमपि मुद्राविरचना
गतिः प्रादक्षिण्यक्रमणमशनाद्याहुतिविधिः ।
प्रणामः संवेशः सुखमखिलमात्मार्पणदृशा
सपर्यापर्यायस्तव भवतु यन्मे विलसितम् ॥

(O Mother!) whatever I articulate, may
that be the saying of thy prayer; may
all my manual craft be the gestures of
your worship; may my walking be going
round you; my eating (and drinking),
offering oblations (to you); may all my
enjoyments be in the spirit of offering
myself to you;—whatever act I do, may
that be synonymous with your worship.

The Saundaryalahari, 27.

अयः स्पर्शे लग्नं सपदि लभते हेमपदवीं
यथा रथ्यापाथः शुचि भवति गङ्गौघमिलितम् ।
तथा तत्तत्पापैरतिमलिनमन्तर्मम यदि
त्वयि प्रेम्णा सक्तं कथमिव न जायेत विमलम् ॥

Just as iron coming into contact with
the philosopher's stone attains at once
the rank of gold and street-water becomes
pure when it gets mixed up with the
flood of the Ganges, even so, how will my
mind, extremely dirty with all sorts of
sin, not become pure if it is united to you
in love?

The Anandalahari, 12.

अयं दानकालस्त्वहं दानपात्रं
भवान्नाथ दाता त्वदन्यं न याचे ।
भवद्भक्तिमेव स्थिरां देहि मह्यं
कृपाशील शंभो कृतार्थोऽस्मि तस्मात् ॥

दरिद्रोऽस्म्यभद्रोऽस्मि भग्नोऽस्मि दूये
विषण्णोऽस्मि सन्नोऽस्मि भिन्नोऽस्मि चाहम् ।
भवान्प्राणिनामन्तरात्माऽसि शंभो
ममाधिं न वेत्सि प्रभो रक्ष मां त्वम् ॥

This is the time to give; I am deserv-
ing of your gift; you are a donor; I beg
not of any beside you; and give me firm
devotion to you alone, O Siva of compassionate nature! With that am I
satisfied.

I am poor, unfortunate, broken, grief-
stricken, done up, torn asunder. O Siva,
you are the inner soul within living beings and (yet) you do not know my
suffering! O Lord, do protect, me.

The Sivabhujanga Stotra, 11, 16.

दृशि स्कन्दमूर्तिः श्रुतौ स्कन्दकीर्तिः
मुखे मे पवित्रं सदा तच्चरित्रम् ।
करे तस्य कृत्यं वपुस्तस्य भृत्यं
गुहे सन्तु लीना ममाशेषभावाः ॥

कलत्रं सुता बन्धुवर्गः पशुर्वा
नरो वाऽथ नारी गृहे ये मदीयाः ।
यजन्तो नमन्तस्तुवन्तो भवन्तं
स्मरन्तश्च ते सन्तु सर्वे कुमार ॥

Skanda's form in my eyes, His glories
in my ears, always His sanctifying ex-
ploits on my lips, His worship on my
hands and His service in my whole body,
—may my entire being be absorbed in
Guha.

Wife, children, kinsmen, cattle, male
or female, everybody belonging to me in
my house,—let all of them, O Kumara, be
worshipping you, bowing to you, prais-
ing you and thinking of you.

The Subrahmanyabhujanga Stotra, 26, 28.

शिलाऽपि त्वदङ्घ्रिक्षमासङ्गिरेणु-
प्रसादाद्धि चैतन्यमाधत्त राम ।
नरस्त्वत्पदद्वन्द्वसेवाविधानात्
सुचैतन्यमेतीति किं चित्रमत्र ॥

O Rama, by the grace of the dust of
your foot-step, even the stone attained
consciousness ; where is the wonder in it
if man attains the consciousness of God-
hood by doing service at your feet?

The Ramabhujanga Stotra, 16.

कदा वा हृषीकानि साम्यं भजेयुः
कदा वा न शत्रुर्न मित्रं भवानि ।
कदा वा दुराशाविषूचीविलोपः
कदा वा मनो मे समूलं विनश्येत् ॥

O Goddess Bhavani, when will (my)
senses attain equanimity ? When will
there be (for me) neither foe nor friend ?
When will the pestilence of evil desire
cease ? When will my mundane menta-
lity perish to its roots ?

The Devibhujanga Stotra, 20.

संसारवृक्षमघबीजमनन्तकर्म-
	शाखाशतं करणपत्रमनङ्गपुष्पम् ।
आरुह्य दुःखफलितं पततो दयालो
	लक्ष्मीनृसिंह मम देहि करावलम्बम् ॥

अन्धस्य मे हृतविवेकमहाधनस्य
	चोरैः प्रभो बलिभिरिन्द्रियनामधेयैः ।
मोहान्धकूपकुहरे विनिपातितस्य
	लक्ष्मीनृसिंह मम देहि करावलम्बम् ॥

O Compassionate Man-Lion God with
Goddess Lakshmi! Give the support of
your hand to me who, having got up the
tree of Samsara, grown from the seed of
sin, with the numerous boughs of Karman, leaves of senses, flower of worldly
enjoyment and fruit of sorrow, is falling
down.

O Man-Lion Lord with G o d d e s s
Lakshmi! Give the support of your hand
to me, the blind man who has been looted
of his great wealth of wisdom by the
violent bandits called senses and has
been fiung (by them) into the deep deso-
late well of delusion.

The Lakshminrisimha Stotra.

Fourth Edition 2000 copies, Aug. 1947.
Printed at Kabeer Printing Works, Triplicane,
M. S. 524, for G. A. Natesan & Co., Madras.

www.pilgrimsbooks.com

*For more details about Pilgrims
and other books published by them
you may visit our website at*
www.pilgrimsbooks.com
or
*for Mail Order and Catalogue
contact us at*

Pilgrims Book House
B. 27/98 A-8 Nawab Ganj Road
Durga Kund Varanasi 221010
Tel. 91-542-2314060
Fax. 91-542-2312456
E-mail: pilgrimsbooks@sify.com

PILGRIMS BOOK HOUSE (New Delhi)
1626, Raj Guru Road Pahar Ganj, Chuna Mandi
New Delhi 110055
Tel: 91-11-23584015, 23584019
E-mail: pilgrim@del2.vsnl.net.in
E-mail: pilgrimsinde@gmail.com

PILGRIMS BOOK HOUSE (Kathmandu)
P O Box 3872, Thamel, Kathmandu, Nepal
Tel: 977-1-4700942,
Off: 977-1-4700919,
Fax: 977-1-4700943
E-mail: pilgrims@wlink.com.np

MORE TITLES ON HINDUISM
FROM PILGRIMS PUBLISHING